# Baby Names

## 2013

Eleanor Turner

white
LADDER

# Acknowledgements

I would like to extend my utmost gratitude to Cerys Owen, Shelley Heck and Michael Turner for their contributions; without them this book would have been much shorter. My thanks are also given to Beth Bishop and Jessica Spencer at Crimson Publishing for their patience and guidance throughout the project. Finally, the greatest thanks go to my children, Owen Henri and Jasper Hugh. I fall more in love with them, and their names, every day.

First edition published by Crimson Publishing in 2011.

ISBN: 978 1 90828 136 4

Typeset by IDSUK (DataConnection) Ltd

Printed and bound in the United States of America by Sheridan Books Inc, Michigan

# Contents

# A note on how to use this book

While the author and publisher acknowledge that baby names vary widely in spelling and pronunciation, this book lists each name only once: under the most common initial and spelling. If a name has an alternate spelling with a different initial, it may be listed under that letter also.

Information relating to statistics and trends in baby names is based on the most recent data at the time of going to press.

# Introduction

Did you know that the name Carter is the most popular name in Iowa, but not in any other state?

Do you know why a certain celebrity couple chose a color for their daughter's name?

Have you considered that the *Twilight* effect on baby names may also be true for *The Hunger Games* phenomenon?

Picking a name for your baby is one of the most enjoyable activities for a new parent, but it's also one of the most daunting. Sometimes choosing the right name is simply a case of hearing one you like and knowing instantly that you've chosen correctly. But for the vast majority of parents the naming game gets far more complicated, and you start trying to please parents, grandparents, friends, and siblings, while trying to avoid names that could be shortened into ridiculous nicknames or that would make for funny initials.

You'll also probably want to choose something unique, but not *too* unique, or common but not *too* common. A name could be inspired by an admired celebrity, a sports star, or an influential historical or political figure. It could also come from the family tree, or follow a current baby-naming trend.

You also need to make sure you love it—you'll have to live with it forever! The possibilities are endless and it's understandable that it can send some parents into panic mode.

Well, never fear. *Baby Names 2013* is here to take you through your options and solve your baby-naming dilemmas. We update it every year, so it always includes the year's most popular names, celebrity choices, and names making a comeback. We've included dozens of lists to provide you with inspiration, and of course, some downright weird names children have been given over the years (usually by celebrities).

Be sure to keep an eye out for all the facts and figures we've got for you—including what names are most popular in each state—so you can either go with the flow . . . or deliberately against it.

Remember, picking a baby name should be fun—so dip in, find some names you like and use the suggestions we've given you to work out if one of them is a winner!

# part one

# 1

# What was hot in 2012?

## The reign of eccentric names

Have you ever raised your eyebrows when you heard a friend's baby name choice? Statistics say you probably have.

Research shows that we are seeing more variation in the names parents are choosing than ever before. In the 1950s, the Top 25 boys' names and the Top 50 girls' names were given to 50% of all babies born in that decade. To reach the same figure now, you would have to include the Top 80 boys' names and the Top 116 girls'. This means that there is a far greater variety of names, spellings, pronunciations, and contracted names than ever before.

One explanation for this is that parents have begun to give their child a name *more* unusual than their own. A parent who has enjoyed their slightly unusual name will feel more confident about giving their offspring an even more unique name. This has been a rising trend since the 1990s, according to a study released in the *Social Psychological and Personality Science* journal—which would make sense, as children who were born in the early 1990s with eccentric names are now having children themselves. If this trend continues into 2013 and beyond, you can be sure that names will get stranger and stranger . . .

Some of the US's quirky baby names during the last year have included Crew, Chaim, Slade, and Thaddeus for boys, and Alaysia, Xiomara, Yamileth, and Zuri for girls.

# Traditional names continue to impress

What's interesting about recent trends, however, is that no matter how many new and unusual names enter the most popular baby name lists each year, you will always see a large number of babies given the same familiar and traditional names of the past. The Top 10 names for both boys and girls seem to stay pretty fixed each year, and 2012 was no different.

The names Jacob, Ethan, and Michael have appeared in the Top 10 boys' names each year since 2002, and the girls' names Isabella, Emma, and Emily have also stayed put. However, last year the name Sophia appeared in the number one slot for baby girls, knocking Isabella off her perch. The name James, which has been the name most often given to baby boys over the last 100 years—an astonishing 4,873,581 little boys, in fact—also remained in the Top 20 at the time of writing in 2012.

## Top 10 baby boy names

1. Jacob
2. Mason
3. William
4. Jayden
5. Noah
6. Michael
7. Ethan
8. Alexander
9. Aiden
10. Daniel

## Top 10 baby girl names

1. Sophia
2. Isabella
3. Emma
4. Olivia
5. Ava
6. Emily
7. Abigail
8. Madison
9. Mia
10. Chloe

Mason was the only new name among the Top 10 for either gender.

We've also seen traditional names re-enter the charts, and a wonderful example of this is the name Lillian. Once the 13th most popular name in the US (in 1911), it had dropped to 485th place by 1978. However, in the last decade it's seen a massive increase in use, and last year clawed its way back to position 22. If this trend continues, next year it will enter the Top 20 for the first time in over 100 years. More traditional names had dropped out of mainstream use by the 1980s and become vastly unpopular, but in the last few years names ending in -a, -ie, and -en have started to see a resurgence, particularly as a spelling option for parents who like the sound of a traditional name but want to give it a modern twist. Other old-fashioned names, such as Henry, Jasper, May, Sophia, and William, have climbed the popularity ranks in the Top 100 lists, along with their alternate spelling options of Henri, Jaz, Mae, Sophie, and Will.

The traditional name for baby boys in some Christian families has often been Noah, which has now become so popular in the US that it entered the Top 10 for the first time in 2009 and last year appeared in 7th place. That's an amazing jump of over 200 places since 1992.

Incredibly, either Jacob or Michael has remained the top choice for parents of newborn baby boys in the US for the last 50 years. While Jacob may have been given to more babies (4.8 million and counting), Michael has claimed the top spot more often (44 times).

## 2012 popular newcomers

| Boys | Girls |
| --- | --- |
| Brantley | Angelique |
| Easton | Adalynn |
| Enzo | Briella |
| Iker | Gia |
| Karter | Kinley |
| Knox | Maci |
| Rhys | Tiana |

# The effects of the entertainment industry

If the last few years have taught us anything about the power of the entertainment industry on baby names, it's that parents are becoming more and more influenced by what they see and hear around them. 2012 was no different, with celebrities such as Adele, Bruno Mars, and Nicole "Snooki" Polizzi dominating the headlines and affecting naming decisions the world over. In the case of Snooki, the name Nicole has actually *decreased* in popularity since *Jersey Shore* became must-watch TV, falling to 116th place last year. Well, no-one ever said influences on baby names had to be positive . . . At the time of writing Snooki was expecting a baby of her own: what she decides to name her child will no doubt be carefully observed by the media and new parents alike.

Adele had one of her most successful years ever in 2012, winning astonishing numbers of awards and selling more records than any other artist in recent years. Because of this, her name was everywhere—and every new parent was exposed to it. It was at its most popular in 1918 and had dropped off the Top 1,000 charts completely by 1970, but in 2011 it suddenly reappeared again. Now sitting comfortably in the 600s, it jumped nearly 300 places in a single year (up from 909 to 627) and it's anyone's guess as to how many children will be named Adele should her third album be as successful as her last one.

The name Bruno saw an increase in popularity last year too, jumping 100 places after the singer Bruno Mars not only released his own solo album, but also contributed to several other Top 10 Billboard hits.

## Growing in popularity

| Boys | Girls |
|------|-------|
| 1. Brantley | 1. Briella |
| 2. Iker | 2. Angelique |
| 3. Maximiliano | 3. Aria |
| 4. Zaiden | 4. Mila |
| 5. Kamden | 5. Elsie |
| 6. Barrett | 6. Nylah |
| 7. Archer | 7. Raelynn |
| 8. Declan | 8. Brynlee |
| 9. Atticus | 9. Olive |
| 10. Nico | 10. June |

Even deceased celebrities are not exempt from baby-naming trends. The sudden death of Whitney Houston in February 2012 inspired many parents to remember the icon by using her name. Last seen in the Top 100 in the 1990s, it surged in popularity last year and is already closing in on the Top 100 again.

The *Twilight* effect describes the amazing influence the Stephenie Meyer series has exerted on baby names. Names such as Isabella (ranked second), Edward (148th but climbing), and Alice (rose from 258th position to 142nd) have all been directly influenced by the vampire stories. Even Cullen, which is merely the last name of the main characters, has been affected—it moved up 70 places in the charts last year. Now that the series is over, it will be interesting to see if this trend continues in years to come.

*The Hunger Games* is the newest book-and-movie phenomenon to impact baby names. However, unlike *Twilight*, where the most popular characters are more likely to see their names on birth certificates, in *The Hunger Games* it's the less well-known or more marginal characters that are influential. The naming website Nameberry announced in 2012 that the name of Rue, a small and sympathetic character in the opening installment of the series, was a popular choice for parents of new baby girls. Also, rather alarmingly, the name of Cato was among the most popular for parents of baby boys—apparently the brutality and cruelty of this character hasn't put people off the name.

The name Elvis dropped out of the Top 1,000 US baby names in 2010, the first year it had not made the list since 1954. However, last year it appeared again in 904th place.

*Game of Thrones*, HBO's runaway success of a fantasy-world drama based on the George R. R. Martin's series of books, has been held accountable for the increase in popularity of the name Arya (or Aria), and the third series of *Downton Abbey* continued to impress parents: the name Violet, for example, from Maggie Smith's acerbic character The Right Honorable Violet Crawley, Countess of Grantham, has proved popular—over 2,500 baby girls were given the name Violet last year.

ABC's show *Revenge* centers on the Grayson family, which might explain why both Grayson and Gray are flying up the charts at the moment. Grayson jumped 50 places in a single year, and Gray appeared in the Top 1,000 for the first time in 2012. NBC's *Smash* might be able to claim responsibility for the newest trend of naming your baby Ivy, after one of the leading characters, but it's more likely that Beyoncé and Jay Z's little girl is the main reason it's suddenly moved up 100 places in the charts to position 266. Keep reading for more on celebrity naming trends.

Colin Firth doesn't like his name, apparently. Last year he was quoted as saying: "Colin is the sort of name you'd give your goldfish for a joke. I once saw an episode of *Blackadder* with a dachshund in it called Colin. It seemed his name alone was supposed to reduce you to fits of laughter."

# Celebrity power

As always, the celebrity world continued to influence choices made by parents in 2012—but we saw a distinct return to more traditional names.

Names beginning with "A" are massively popular with celebrities at the moment. Names such as Agnes (Jennifer Connelly and Paul Bettany's daughter), Aleph (Natalie Portman and Benjamin Millepied's son), Arthur (Selma Blair and Jason Bleick's son), Arlo (Johnny Knoxville's son), and Adalaide (Katherine Heigl and Josh Kelley's adopted daughter) were fairly big hits with non-celebrities too: Agnes, which hasn't been seen in the Top 1,000 since the 1970s, has suddenly reappeared.

Although celebrities are often known for choosing highly original (or simply weird) names for their children, new arrivals in the last year or so have actually been given fairly normal names by their standards. However, there is definitely a trend for choosing old-fashioned names— celebrities are certainly showing they're not afraid of names that the world hasn't used widely since World War II. Babies were named Pearl (Jack Osbourne and Lisa Stelly), Delilah (Kimberley Stewart and Benicio Del Toro), Henry (Emily Deschanel and David Hornsby), Hattie (Tori Spelling and Dean McDermott), Ethel (Lily Allen and Sam Cooper), and Mabel Ray (Bruce Willis and Emma Heming Willis). In the case of Tori Spelling, it's claimed she picked all the names of her children according to people who'd been influential in her life—for daughter Hattie Margaret, this meant being named after Spelling's childhood nanny. Now Spelling has announced her fourth pregnancy (due in September 2012), it will be interesting to see what name she chooses this time around, and why.

An Israeli couple have called their baby girl "Like" after the Facebook button. Their other children are called Pie and Vash, which means honey.

## Celebrity babies of the last year

Arlo (Johnny Knoxville and Naomi Nelson, Oct 2011)

Giulia (Carla Bruni-Sarkozy and Nicholas Sarkozy, Oct 2011)

Hattie Margaret (Tori Spelling and Dean McDermott, Oct 2011)

Tristan Milos (Vanessa and Donald Trump Jr., Oct 2011)

Mason Evan (Monyetta Shaw and Ne-Yo, Oct 2011)

Marcelo Alejandro (Ali Landry and Alejandro Gomez Monteverde, Oct 2011)

Ethel Mary (Lily Allen and Sam Cooper, Nov 2011)

Elise (Celia Walden and Piers Morgan, Nov 2011)

Russell Wallace (Mary Elizabeth Ellis and Charlie Day, Dec 2011)

Varro (Essence Atkins and Jaime Mendez, Dec 2011)

Willa Lou (Keri Russell and Shane Deary, Dec 2011)

Kaya Emory (Lindsay Davenport and Jonathan Leach, Jan 2012)

Maxwell Lue (Lindsay Sloane and Dar Rollins, Jan 2012)

Blue Ivy (Beyoncé Knowles and Jay Z, Jan 2012)

Beatrice Jean (Bryce Dallas Howard and Seth
Gabel, Jan 2012)

Micah Emmanuel (Sarah Drew and Peter Lanfer,
Jan 2012)

Exton Elias (Susan and Robert Downey Jr., Feb 2012)

Estelle Silvia Ewa Mary (Sweden's Crown Princess
Victoria and Prince Daniel, Feb 2012)

Samuel (Jennifer Garner and Ben Affleck,
Mar 2012)

Joshua (Kimberly and James Van Der Beek
(Mar 2012)

Jackson (Charlize Theron, adopted Mar 2012)

Luca Cruz (Hilary Duff and Eric Comrie, Mar 2012)

Mabel Ray (Bruce Willis and Emma Heming Willis,
Apr 2012)

Pearl (Jack Osbourne and Lisa Stelly, Apr 2012)

Hawkins (Tony Roma and Candice Crawford,
Apr 2012)

Adalaide Marie Hope (Katherine Heigl and Josh Kelley,
adopted Apr 2012)

Gloria Ray (Maggie Gullenhaal and Peter Saarsgaard,
Apr 2012)

Maxwell Drew (Jessica Simpson and Eric Johnson,
May 2012)

Noah Phoenix (Alessandra Ambrosio and Jamie
Mazurboy, May 2012)

Keeva Jane (Alyson Hannigan and Alexis
Denisof, May 2012)

Of course, celebrities were not entirely sensible last year and there was the usual selection of unique and odd-sounding names that we have come to love and expect. Beyoncé and husband Jay Z have chosen perhaps the oddest name for their daughter: Blue Ivy. According to the media, "Blue" was chosen because it's daddy Jay Z's favorite color; "Ivy" has several proposed meanings, starting with the fact it looks like the Roman number IV, which means "4." The number four is significant to the couple for several reasons—they were married on 4/4 (April 4th), they both have birthdays on the fourth of the month, and Beyoncé's fourth album was called, inspiringly, "4." Shame they didn't keep it for their fourth child really . . .

Beyoncé might be on to something: Blue Ivy is the sixth celebrity child to be named after the color. Other "blue" parents include Cher, John Travolta, The Edge, Geri Halliwell, and Alicia Silverstone.

Numbers as names didn't escape other celebrity couples either: Victoria and David Beckham gave their highly-anticipated daughter Harper, the middle name Seven. For more on middle name trends, see page 57.

Mariah Carey and Nick Cannon's twins followed the trend of crazy celebrity baby names—baby girl Monroe was named after Marilyn Monroe, and Moroccan Scott was named after the Moroccan Room in his parent's penthouse, where Nick proposed. Scott is also Nick's middle name. Mariah sent fans into a frenzy when she strung her name announcement out for hours, getting her followers on Twitter to guess the names.

# Crazy celebrity baby names of recent years

Bingham Hawn (Kate Hudson and Matthew Bellamy—also parents to Ryder)

Bluebell Madonna (Geri Halliwell)

Blue Ivy (Beyoncé Knowles and Jay Z)

Bronx Mowgli (Ashlee Simpson and Pete Wentz)

Buddy Bear Maurice (Jules and Jamie Oliver—also parents to Daisy Boo, Poppy Honey, and Petal Blossom Rainbow)

Cosima Violet (Claudia Schiffer and Matthew Vaughn—also parents to Caspar and Clementine)

Egypt Dauode Dean (Alicia Keys and Swizz Beatz)

Ever Imre (Alanis Morissette and Mario Treadway)

Harper Seven (Victoria and David Beckham—also parents to Brooklyn, Romeo, and Cruz)

Ickhyd (M.I.A. and Ben Brewer)

Kahekili (Evangeline Lilly and Norman Kali)

Moses (Gwyneth Paltrow and Chris Martin—also parents to Apple)

Shiloh Nouvel (Brad Pitt and Angelina Jolie—also parents to Zahara, Maddox, Pax, Knox, and Vivienne)

Sparrow (Nicole Richie and Joel Madden—also parents to Harlow Winter)

Spike (Mike Myers and Kelly Tisdale)

Sunday Rose (Nicole Kidman and Keith Urban)

Zuma Nesta Rock (Gwen Stefani and Gavin Rossdale—also parents to Kingston)

# State differences

What's interesting about US baby name statistics is that there is such variety in the popularity of names across different states and territories . . .

- The name Parker appears as one of the most popular boys' names only in Wyoming, while the names Isabella and Emma appear in almost every single Top 5 girls' list in the country.

- While the names William and Jacob were popular across the board, only parents in Maine and Montana were more likely to name their baby boys Wyatt.

- Baby girls were predominantly given names such as Sophia, Emma, Isabella, or Madison except in South Dakota where Brooklyn made the Top 5.

The most popular name in Iowa is currently Carter, even though it was only given to 195 babies.

It makes sense that Spanish names are more popular where there is a higher Hispanic population, and this is likely to be in those border states in the South: the name Angel, for example, appears in Texas, Arizona, and Puerto Rico's Top 5 names for boys. It seems as though geography can have a major impact on baby-naming decisions, and population density can certainly change the rankings.

What was hot in 2012?

Find your state from the lists below—and make sure your baby won't have another ten Isabellas or Jacobs in their class!

# Top five girls' names by state

| State | Rank 1 | Rank 2 | Rank 3 | Rank 4 | Rank 5 |
|---|---|---|---|---|---|
| Alabama | Emma | Ava | Madison | Olivia | Isabella |
| Alaska | Olivia | Emma | Isabella | Madison | Sophia |
| Arizona | Sophia | Isabella | Emma | Emily | Mia |
| Arkansas | Emma | Isabella | Addison | Madison | Abigail |
| California | Sophia | Isabella | Emily | Mia | Emma |
| Colorado | Olivia | Sophia | Emma | Isabella | Abigail |
| Connecticut | Sophia | Isabella | Olivia | Ava | Emma |
| Delaware | Sophia | Olivia | Ava | Emma | Emily |
| Dist. of Columbia | Sophia | Ava | Elizabeth | Olivia | Sofia |
| Florida | Isabella | Sophia | Emma | Olivia | Emily |
| Georgia | Emma | Isabella | Madison | Olivia | Ava |
| Hawaii | Sophia | Olivia | Chloe | Emma | Isabella |
| Idaho | Emma | Sophia | Olivia | Ava | Emily |
| Illinois | Sophia | Olivia | Isabella | Emma | Emily |
| Indiana | Emma | Olivia | Ava | Sophia | Isabella |
| Iowa | Emma | Olivia | Sophia | Ava | Addison |
| Kansas | Sophia | Emma | Olivia | Isabella | Ava |
| Kentucky | Emma | Isabella | Sophia | Olivia | Addison |
| Louisiana | Ava | Emma | Isabella | Sophia | Olivia |
| Maine | Emma | Sophia | Isabella | Olivia | Ava |
| Maryland | Sophia | Olivia | Isabella | Madison | Ava |

19

# Baby Names 2013

| State | Rank 1 | Rank 2 | Rank 3 | Rank 4 | Rank 5 |
|---|---|---|---|---|---|
| Massachusetts | Sophia | Olivia | Isabella | Emma | Ava |
| Michigan | Olivia | Sophia | Emma | Isabella | Ava |
| Minnesota | Olivia | Sophia | Emma | Ava | Isabella |
| Mississippi | Madison | Emma | Ava | Addison | Olivia |
| Missouri | Emma | Sophia | Olivia | Ava | Isabella |
| Montana | Emma | Madison | Olivia | Ava | Harper |
| Nebraska | Emma | Sophia | Olivia | Ava | Ella |
| Nevada | Sophia | Isabella | Olivia | Emily | Emma |
| New Hampshire | Sophia | Olivia | Emma | Ava | Isabella |
| New Jersey | Sophia | Isabella | Olivia | Ava | Emily |
| New Mexico | Sophia | Isabella | Mia | Nevaeh | Emma |
| New York | Sophia | Isabella | Olivia | Emma | Ava |
| North Carolina | Emma | Ava | Olivia | Isabella | Sophia |
| North Dakota | Emma | Ava | Sophia | Olivia | Harper |
| Ohio | Emma | Sophia | Ava | Olivia | Isabella |
| Oklahoma | Emma | Sophia | Isabella | Olivia | Ava |
| Oregon | Sophia | Emma | Olivia | Ava | Isabella |
| Pennsylvania | Sophia | Emma | Ava | Olivia | Isabella |
| Rhode Island | Sophia | Olivia | Isabella | Emma | Ava |
| South Carolina | Madison | Emma | Isabella | Olivia | Ava |
| South Dakota | Ava | Emma | Olivia | Sophia | Brooklyn |
| Tennessee | Emma | Isabella | Ava | Olivia | Madison |
| Texas | Sophia | Isabella | Emma | Mia | Emily |
| Utah | Olivia | Sophia | Emma | Lily | Abigail |
| Vermont | Emma | Olivia | Sophia | Ava | Isabella |
| Virginia | Sophia | Emma | Olivia | Isabella | Abigail |
| Washington | Sophia | Olivia | Emma | Isabella | Emily |
| West Virginia | Isabella | Emma | Madison | Sophia | Addison |
| Wisconsin | Sophia | Emma | Ava | Olivia | Isabella |
| Wyoming | Emma | Olivia | Addison | Sophia | Isabella |

# Top five boys' names by state

| State | Rank 1 | Rank 2 | Rank 3 | Rank 4 | Rank 5 |
|---|---|---|---|---|---|
| Alabama | William | Mason | James | Jacob | John |
| Alaska | Mason | James | William | Liam | Ethan |
| Arizona | Jacob | Anthony | Daniel | Michael | Ethan |
| Arkansas | William | Jacob | Mason | Aiden | Noah |
| California | Jacob | Daniel | Jayden | Anthony | Matthew |
| Colorado | Liam | Mason | Noah | Elijah | William |
| Connecticut | Alexander | Michael | Mason | Ryan | Jacob |
| Delaware | Michael | Mason | Ryan | William | Noah |
| Dist. of Columbia | William | Alexander | Daniel | James | Christopher |
| Florida | Jayden | Jacob | Daniel | Noah | Michael |
| Georgia | William | Christopher | Mason | Joshua | Jayden |
| Hawaii | Noah | Mason | Elijah | Aiden | Ethan |
| Idaho | Mason | Jacob | Liam | Benjamin | Alexander |
| Illinois | Alexander | Michael | Jacob | Noah | Daniel |
| Indiana | Mason | Liam | Elijah | Noah | William |
| Iowa | Carter | Mason | Owen | Noah | Jacob |
| Kansas | Mason | William | Jacob | Ethan | Jackson |
| Kentucky | William | Mason | Elijah | Jacob | Brayden |
| Louisiana | Mason | Jayden | Aiden | William | Landon |
| Maine | Mason | Liam | Jacob | Benjamin | Wyatt |
| Maryland | Mason | Jacob | Michael | Ethan | Ryan |
| Massachusetts | William | Benjamin | Jacob | Michael | Ryan |
| Michigan | Mason | Jacob | Noah | Logan | Liam |
| Minnesota | Mason | William | Jacob | Liam | Benjamin |
| Mississippi | William | James | Jayden | John | Christopher |
| Missouri | Mason | William | Noah | Jacob | Liam |
| Montana | Mason | Liam | Wyatt | Jacob | Noah |
| Nebraska | Mason | Jackson | William | Alexander | Jacob |

# Baby Names 2013

| State | Rank 1 | Rank 2 | Rank 3 | Rank 4 | Rank 5 |
|-------|--------|--------|--------|--------|--------|
| Nevada | Anthony | Jacob | Daniel | Mason | Jayden |
| New Hampshire | Mason | Logan | Liam | Jackson | Noah |
| New Jersey | Michael | Ryan | Anthony | Jayden | Jacob |
| New Mexico | Jacob | Elijah | Michael | Aiden | Noah |
| New York | Michael | Jacob | Jayden | Matthew | Joseph |
| North Carolina | William | Mason | Jacob | Elijah | Noah |
| North Dakota | Mason | Carter | Jacob | Liam | Ethan |
| Ohio | Mason | Jacob | Noah | William | Liam |
| Oklahoma | William | Mason | Jacob | Noah | Elijah |
| Oregon | Mason | Liam | Logan | Jacob | Alexander |
| Pennsylvania | Mason | Michael | Jacob | Logan | Ryan |
| Rhode Island | Mason | Michael | Benjamin | William | Jayden |
| South Carolina | William | Mason | Jayden | James | Aiden |
| South Dakota | Mason | Carter | William | Logan | Elijah |
| Tennessee | William | Mason | Elijah | Jacob | James |
| Texas | Jacob | Jayden | Daniel | Jose | David |
| Utah | Mason | William | James | Jacob | Samuel |
| Vermont | Liam | William | Mason | Carter | Benjamin |
| Virginia | William | Jacob | Mason | Noah | Ethan |
| Washington | Mason | Liam | Alexander | Jacob | Ethan |
| West Virginia | Mason | Jacob | Landon | Noah | Aiden |
| Wisconsin | Mason | Liam | William | Logan | Owen |
| Wyoming | William | Jacob | Jackson | Parker | Liam |

## Banned names around the world

@—China

Akuma (meaning "devil")—Japan

Anus—Denmark

Chow Tow (meaning "smelly head")—Malaysia

Dalmata (meaning "Dalmatian")—Italy

Gesher (meaning "bridge")—Norway

Monkey—Denmark

Ovnis (meaning "UFO")—Portugal

Q—Sweden

Sor Chai (meaning "insane")—Malaysia

Stompy—Germany

# 2

# What does 2013 hold for baby names?

## Will these trends continue?

Looking forward to 2013, we predict the trend for choosing either old fashioned or unique names will continue. The Top 10 names will probably go largely unchanged for both boys and girls, but we may become even more varied in the names we give our children, and not just stick to the same safe names. There may also be a backlash against very popular names, as parents opt to not give their child the same name as four or five of their potential school friends.

As parents grow more globally aware and the demographics of North America change, we may see more culturally and ethnically diverse names appearing in these lists, such as Raza and Mekhi. This has already started to happen with the Italian name Giuliana, which jumped up a massive 382 positions in the last two years, from 705 to 323. (This may also have had something to do with the *E! News* host Giuliana Rancic's tumultuous year, which saw her battle breast cancer and have a child via a gestational carrier surrogate—all of which was recorded for posterity on her reality-TV show, *Giuliana and Bill*.)

Parents may also start looking further back into their family trees for inspiration, giving rise to many more African (Iman, Kwame), Asian (Mali, Thao), Scandinavian (Karita, Larson), and Middle English names (Avery, Tate). Our heritage is such a hugely important part of life in the US that it would be very appropriate for parents to choose the name of an ancestor for their new baby.

In general, American parents prefer to give their children full-length names rather than shortened versions or nicknames, and this trend doesn't show much sign of stopping. Elizabeth (11th) appears higher up the charts than Ellie (97th), and Robert (61st) is much higher than Bobby (688th). The nickname "Bob" doesn't even rank in the SSA's Top 1,000! We see this over and over again: Leonardo (149th) is more popular than Leo (167th), Allison (40th) is higher up than Allie (198th) or Ally (674th), and Eve (546th) is much further down the charts than Evelyn (24th).

However, it must be said that in some cases, picking short versions of traditional names is on the upswing. The name Lily (15th last year), for example, is a shortened version of Lillian (22nd), while Max (96th) is a shortened version of either Maxwell (134th) or Maximilian (433rd); both of these shorter names are clearly more popular than the longer ones. In Europe this is particularly fashionable right now, so perhaps in 2013 we will see much more of this trend, and even a few surprises.

## Predicted 2013 Top 10 baby names

| Boys | Girls |
|---|---|
| 1. Jacob | 1. Sophia |
| 2. Mason | 2. Isabella |
| 3. Jayden | 3. Emma |
| 4. William | 4. Ava |
| 5. Michael | 5. Olivia |
| 6. Noah | 6. Emily |
| 7. Daniel | 7. Abigail |
| 8. Aiden | 8. Madison |
| 9. Alexander | 9. Chloe |
| 10. Ethan | 10. Mia |

# 2013 events

Other influences on the names parents choose in 2013 may come from the worlds of sport, politics, and celebrity.

After the hugely publicized London Olympics and Paralympics in 2012, sporting events in 2013 seem a little tame by comparison. However, the winners of the 109th World Series, Superbowl XLVII (hosted this time in New Orleans), the All-Star Stanley Cup game, and even the Tour de France, may have an impact—you never know! Ben

Roethlisberger, quarterback for the Pittsburgh Steelers, saw his name jump to position 20 in the US national statistics the same year his team won their sixth Superbowl title in 2009.

The eyes of soccer fans will be resting on the outcome of the Africa Cup of Nations, hosted this time in South Africa. Successful soccer stars often have babies named after them, with names such as Wayne (Rooney), Thierry (Henry), and Landon (Donovan) all peaking in popularity during sporting events. Perhaps some emerging African players will also follow this trend.

The third World Baseball Classic is set to take place in 2013, after being postponed from 2012 to avoid conflicting with the Olympics. While the US has not yet entered a team for the qualifying round, for baseball fans this will still be worth watching. Japan has won the last two Classics, and star player Ichiro Suzuki has many babies named after him in his home country. It's possible American parents will follow suit, particularly those of Asian heritage.

One major set of events planned for 2013 is more space exploration. The People's Republic of China will launch its first unmanned space flight to the Moon, and the US is sending a new explorer to Mars, called MAVEN, and another to Venus. It's a possibility that key players in these events will become famous, which will undoubtedly affect baby name statistics.

2013 will also be a fairly important year politically. At the time of writing the Presidential election had not taken place, but whatever the outcome and whomever the President is as of January 1st, 2013, it is sure to be the result of a bitter and hard-won political battle. Politicians have a hazy history of influencing baby names—it's not true to say that children are frequently named after presidents; the name George actually declined in popularity during President George W. Bush's term. President Barack Obama's name has yet to enter even the Top 1,000 in the US, and UK Prime Minister David Cameron's first name has dropped 22 places in the last 10 years. However, David Cameron's *last* name has appeared in the Top 60 pretty consistently over the last 20 years, and shows no sign of dropping out in the near future.

Will children born in 2013 be called Willard, or Mitt, after Republican candidate Mitt Romney? History suggests not, because neither name has been seen in the Top 1,000 since 1989.

Interestingly, there is a trend of naming babies after the *children* of politicians—Barack Obama's daughters are named Maliyah and Sasha, and a variation of both of these appear in the Top 100 names for girls. In the UK, when David Cameron's newborn daughter was named Florence in 2010, the media went wild, and a flurry of parents started choosing this name for their baby girls shortly after. In fact, it jumped an astonishing 26 places the year she was born, and has moved up 108 places in the last ten years. Even Florrie, which is a popular nickname for Florence, has appeared in the charts for the first time ever.

Sometimes the phenomenon of naming babies after the children of politicians doesn't even have to mean the successful ones: Sarah Palin's attempt to become the Vice-President in 2008 fixed the world's eyes upon her, and led to her five children becoming somewhat famous in their own right. Her daughter Bristol, who competed in the 11th season of *Dancing with the Stars* in 2010, saw her name enter the Top 1,000 for the first time in 2009, and Piper, Palin's fourth child, has seen her name steadily increase in popularity since the family came to the nation's attention in 2007.

# Significant dates in 2013

Significant anniversaries can potentially influence baby names. In 2013 this includes the 50th anniversary of Martin Luther King Jr.'s iconic "I Have A Dream" speech, 100 years since the birth of civil rights activist Rosa Parks, the 150th birthday of actor/director Constantin Stanislavsky, the 200th year since Jane Austen's *Pride and Prejudice* was published, and 200 years since the births of composers Richard Wagner and Giuseppe Verdi.

Other anniversaries include 25 years since the Lockerbie bombing, the 40th anniversary of Concorde's first non-stop flight across the Atlantic (and the 10th anniversary of their last . . .), 90 years since Tutankhamun's tomb was unsealed by Harold Carter, 125 years since Jack the Ripper first struck, the 150th anniversary of Abraham Lincoln's Gettysburg Address, the 175th anniversary of the coronation of Queen Victoria, and the 400th year since the original Shakespearean Globe Theatre burned to the ground.

A significant anniversary year for women's rights, 2013 includes the 100th anniversary of UK suffragette Emily Davison's death (she was killed by jumping in front of the

King's horse), the 100th anniversary of all women's suffrage in Norway, and 130 years since New Zealand granted every woman the right to vote (thanks to women such as Kate Sheppard and Mary Ann Müller). It's also been 50 years since Afghanistan, Iran, Kenya, and Morocco each allowed equal political rights to women.

Don't be surprised, therefore, if names linked to these anniversaries start becoming popular. As the media at large begins to broadcast these significant dates, names such as Martin (Luther King Jr.), Rosa (Parks), Constantin (Stanislavsky), Jane (Austen), Elizabeth (Bennet), Darcy, Richard (Wagner), Giuseppe (Verdi), Harold (Carter), Jack (the Ripper), Abraham (Lincoln), Victoria (Queen), Emily (Davison), Kate (Sheppard), and Mary Ann (Müller) will start to be considered by parents as potential options for their baby names. And, the more heavily they're promoted, the more frequently they'll get used.

## 2013 anniversary names

| Boys | Girls |
| --- | --- |
| Abraham | Ann |
| Constantin | Elizabeth |
| Darcy | Emily |
| Giuseppe | Jane |
| Harold | Kate |
| Jack | Mary |
| Martin | Rosa |
| Richard | Victoria |

# The influence of the entertainment industry

Pop culture will be perhaps the most prominent influence on baby names in the coming year. Celebrity couples expecting babies in late 2012 and in 2013 include Sarah Michelle Gellar, Nick Lachey, Uma Thurman, and Drew Barrymore. If the names these celebrities choose are particularly noteworthy, they may well influence the choices made by the general population. For more on how celebrity baby names affect current trends, see page 13.

Web-based newspaper The Huffington Post released an article in 2012 that broke down the names chosen by celebrities into common categories. Of the 50+ names they analyzed, every single one fell into one of 10 fields: authors (e.g., Harper, David Beckham's daughter), cities (Savannah, Marcia Cross's daughter), colors (Blue Ivy, Beyoncé's daughter), comic book characters (Kal-El, Nicolas Cage's son), countries (Morroccan, Mariah Carey's son), fruits (Clementine, Ethan Hawke's daughter), New York boroughs (Bronx, Ashlee Simpson's son), music icons (Louis, Sandra Bullock's son), old Hollywood (Monroe, Mariah Carey's daughter), and Shakespearean characters (Exton, Robert Downey Jr.'s son). It's quite impressive that ALL the celebrity names they analyzed slotted so neatly into the same categories!

❝ Words have meaning and names have power. ❞

Anoymous

## Expected new arrivals in 2012/2013

Elizabeth Berkley and Greg Lauren (Summer 2012)

Vanessa and Nick Lachey (Summer 2012)

Kristin Cavallari and Jay Cutler (Summer 2012)

Neve Campbell and JJ Field (Summer 2012)

Sienna Miller and Tom Sturridge (Summer 2012)

Molly Sims and Scott Stuber (Summer 2012)

Giuliana and Bill Rancic (Summer 2012)

Drew Barrymore and Will Kopelman (Fall 2012)

Reese Witherspoon and Jim Toth (Fall 2012)

Uma Thurman and Arpad Busson (Fall 2012)

Nicole "Snooki" Polizzi and Jionni LaValle (Fall 2012)

Anna Paquin and Stephen Moyer (Fall 2012)

Melissa Joan Hart and Mark Wilkerson (Fall 2012)

Megan Fox and Brian Austin Green (Winter 2012)

Tori Spelling and Dean McDermott (Winter 2012)

Natalie and Taylor Hanson (Winter 2012)

Sarah Michelle Gellar and Freddie Prinze Jr. (Winter 2012)

What's exciting about pop culture and the entertainment industry is how everything, from films and TV to books and blogs, can shape the world of baby names.

The year 2013 looks set to be the year of the remake, reboot, and sequel. Upcoming movies in 2013 include a new instalment in the Wizard of Oz franchise, *Oz: The Great and Powerful*; a new Superman movie, *Superman: Man of Steel*; the next episode in Stieg Larsson's Girl trilogy, *The Girl Who Played With Fire*; another Lara Croft sequel;

*Iron Man 3*; *The Smurfs 2*; *Despicable Me 2*; *Scary Movie 5*; and new versions of *Dirty Dancing*, *Robocop*, *Teenage Mutant Ninja Turtles*, and *Jurassic Park*. It will also be the year of the classic fairy tale, with *Hansel and Gretel: Witch Hunters*, *Jack the Giant Killer* and a new Disney movie called *King of the Elves* in the works.

It's likely that *Oz: The Great and Powerful* will be a massive hit, and its stars—James Franco, Mila Kunis, Rachel Weisz, and Michelle Williams—will also be in huge demand in 2013. However, because the character of Dorothy isn't actually in this film (it's a prequel to *The Wizard of Oz*), that name will probably not have as big an impact as it did in 1939 when the original was released. At that time it was the 9th most popular girls' name, but has since dropped to 982nd place. Perhaps the name "Oz" will become a sudden runaway success this time around? (Not a single baby boy was given that name last year though, so perhaps not . . .)

It's great when movie studios release films that are remakes and sequels, because you can look back at when the original versions were released and see how baby name trends were affected at the time. For example, when the original *Lara Croft: Tomb Raider* movie was released in 2001, the name Lara jumped an impressive 200 places between 2000 and 2002. Last year it sat at position 924, so it's entirely possible it will appear in the Top 500 for the first time in over 20 years once the new film is released in 2013. The same can be said of the characters in Stieg Larsson's Girl trilogy: in Sweden, the name Mikeal has been steadily growing in popularity over the last five years, so it will be interesting to see what happens next. (Incidentally, if you want to take a look at how other countries around the world display their baby name statistics, I highly recommend starting with Sweden's official website. I have yet to find a country that presents its figures in a clearer or more user-friendly format.)

Popular TV programs set to air in 2013 include several exciting-looking dramas. *To Appomatox*, which follows the lives of Civil War generals, looks set to be a hit and stars Rob Lowe, amongst others. David Fincher returns to the small screen with his *House of Cards* series, starring Kevin Spacey as Francis Urquhart, alongside Kate Mara and Robin Wright, and there are several comedy shows returning for new seasons. *Big Bang Theory*, *Mike & Molly*, *How I Met Your Mother*, and *2 Broke Girls* will all reappear in 2013.

---

## Rising stars

| Boys | Girls |
|------|-------|
| Francis | Gretel |
| Hansel | Kate |
| Jack | Lara |
| Mikael | Lisbeth |
| Rob | Robin |

---

Reality series will continue to influence our decisions—the name Khloe (spelt with a K) jumped in popularity after the *Keeping Up with the Kardashians* star began her own reality show with husband Lamar Odom in 2011, and now that Khloe's sister Kourtney has had her second baby with boyfriend Scott Disick, the name she has chosen for her daughter, Penelope Scotland, may be prove to be a trend in 2013. Even the SSA has admitted that the astonishing rise of the name Mason from twelfth position to second can be attributed to Kourtney Kardashian, saying in their press release "Some may attribute this year's rise to number two to reality TV star Kourtney Kardashian's son." It's quite impressive that a single baby can have that much impact on the baby-naming world . . .

One of *Glee's* most talked-about characters, Quinn, named her baby Beth. However, while the name Beth might not have risen in popularity recently, the name Quinn definitely has! It jumped 300 places last year, up from position 487 the year before.

# 3

# How to choose a name

## Top tips on choosing a name

- **Fall in love with the name(s) you've chosen.** If you plough through this book and none of them jump off the page at you, then you probably haven't found the right one yet. Likewise, if a relative, friend, or even your spouse suggests a name and you wrinkle your nose up every time you hear it, it's also not the name for your baby. Pick a name that makes you smile because if you love it, hopefully your child will too.

- **Don't listen to other people.** Sometimes, grandparents and friends will offer "advice" to you during this time which may not always be welcome. This is worth bearing in mind if you've fallen in love with a name and it's either slightly unusual or doesn't follow the set pattern your partner's family have used for the last 50 years. Sharing your choice of name with other people can lead them to criticize it, which you'd probably rather not hear if you've got your heart set on it. Also, if you're bucking with tradition and don't plan on calling your newborn after their great-great-great-grandfather, keep it a secret until after the birth. Trust your own instincts and remember: no one will really care once they see your baby. Its name will simply be its name.

- **Find a name with meaning.** When my parents discovered they were expecting a baby, they sought out possibilities that *meant* something. Both interested in history, they eventually settled on naming their three daughters after Queens of England (Alexandra, Eleanor, and Victoria), hoping to fill their children's souls with a sense of pride and importance. It worked, because throughout our lives we have all felt a duty to do our names justice in the modern world. Having a name that has a back story helps your child understand their significance in the world, so whether you name them after a religious saint or prophet, an important political figure, or a hero in a Greek tragedy, ensure they know where their name came from. They may just be inspired to be as great as their namesake.

- **Have fun.** Picking out names should be a fun process. Laughing at the ones you'd never dream of choosing can really help you narrow it down to the ones you would.

You can also experiment with different spellings, pronunciations, or variations of names you like, or go to places where you might feel inspired.

- **Expand your mind.** Don't rule out the weird ones just yet! As a teenager I went to school with a girl named Siam. Her parents had conceived her on a honeymoon trip to Thailand and given her the country's old name as a result. She loved growing up and having an unusual name, as I'm sure Egypt (Alicia Keys and Swizz Beatz's son) and Bronx Wentz (Ashley Simpson and Pete Wentz's son) do too. Also, don't be afraid to play around with spellings and pronunciations, even if the results are a little less than conformist. The name Madison, for example, could be spelt Maddison, Madyson, Maddiesun, or even Maddeesunn if you so choose, although you might want to be careful you don't saddle your child with an impossible name to spell, pronounce, *and* fit onto a passport application form.

The shortest baby names are only two letters long (Al, Ed, Jo, and Ty), but the longest could be any length imaginable. Popular 11 letter-long names include Bartholomew, Christopher, Constantine, and Maximillian.

- **Try it out.** While you're pregnant, talk to your baby and address it using a variety of your favorite names to see if it responds. There are numerous stories of names being chosen because the baby kicked when it was called Charlie or Aisha, but was suspiciously silent when it was called Dexter or Mildred, so see if it has a preference! Try writing names down and sticking them to your fridge, or saying one out loud enough times to see if you ever get sick of it.

- **Do NOT pick the name of an ex.** No matter how lovely Brad Pitt thought the name "Jennifer" was, it's unlikely Angelina Jolie would have allowed him to use it for one of their daughters. The same is probably true of picking the names of your friends' exes. They are unlikely to thank you if they have to say a name they loathe repeatedly. Just steer clear of any names you know will have problems for other people, paying particular attention to your partner and loved ones.

- **What if you can't agree?** This is probably the trickiest problem in the baby-naming process to solve. It's wise to research a number of names you and your partner are both interested in and make a point of discussing your reasons for liking or disliking them long before the baby is due to be born. The labor and delivery room is probably not the best time to argue as you'll both be tired, emotional, and at least one of you will be in pain. Avoid sticking to your guns on a name one of you really isn't happy with because it might lead to resentment down the line, with your baby caught in the middle. You could try compromising and picking two middle names so you both have a name in there you love, or you could each have five names you're allowed to "veto" but no more. Whichever way you go about it, it is important that you both eventually agree on the name you are giving your baby, even if it means losing out on that one you've had your heart set on for a while.

## Popular names from the past

| Boys | Girls |
|------|-------|
| Abraham | Agatha |
| Arthur | Bertha |
| Edmund | Clara |
| Emmett | Edith |
| Franklin | Gladys |
| Gilbert | Mabel |
| Jasper | Pearl |
| Neville | Theodora |
| Percival | Wilhelmina |
| Vincent | Winifred |

# Think to the future

*"Always end the name of your child with a vowel, so that when you yell the name will carry."*

Bill Cosby

One important aspect of naming your child is thinking ahead to their future. Will the name you've chosen stand the test of time? Will names popular in 2013 remain popular in 2040? Will they be able to confidently enter a room and give a crucial business presentation with an awkward or unpronounceable name? Will they be able to hand their business card over to a potential client without that client looking bemused every time? Even on a smaller scale, can they survive the potential minefields of elementary school and junior high with a name that could be easily shortened to something embarrassing?

Would you want to try catching criminals as Sheriff Apple Blossom or have other politicians take you seriously with a name like Senator Lil' Kim Scarlett? You don't want to give your child a name that they just cannot live with for the rest of their lives, so make your choice based on what's appropriate for a child as well as an adult. To make this easier you might want to choose a longer name that can be shortened or extended as your child desires.

Singer/actor Matt Willis dealt with this very problem in November 2011, when he announced the birth of his new baby son on Twitter. Willis wrote: "I have a son and his name is Ace!" When a follower made a crack about the name, asking if the middle name would be "Ventura," after the popular Jim Carrey character, Willis responded with: "Nearly! Went for Billy so if he wants to be like a f\*\*king banker or something he can use that instead!"

## Names that should be banned

Anna Banana Baptista
Benson and Hedges (twins)
Ford Mustang
Hairy Berry
Kaos
Laxative Thomas
Masport and Mower (twins)

Midnight Chardonnay
Number 16 Bus Shelter
Spiral Cicada
Superman (changed from 4Real)
Violence

French law prohibits all names other than those on an approved list. However, in 2012 French courts allowed one couple to call their child "Daemon" after a vampire character in the TV show *True Blood*—the first such deviation from the approved list in a decade.

## Stereotypes—true or false?

Will the name you choose actually affect your child's life? Will names that seem clever make your child brainier? Will names with positive meanings make your child into a happier person? The answer is . . . possibly.

Some experts believe that parents who choose inspirational names for their offspring (Destiny, Serenity, Unique) or names of products they would like to own (Armani, Jaguar, Mercedes) are projecting a future onto their child for them to aspire to, and therefore help shape their child's life. There's no scientific evidence to prove that this actually works—but feel free to give it a go!

## Inspirational names

| | |
|---|---|
| Destiny | Joy |
| Happy | Peace |
| Heaven | Serenity |
| Hope | Unique |
| Innocence | Unity |

## Aspirational names

| | |
|---|---|
| Armani | Ferrari |
| Aston | Jaguar |
| Bugatti | Mercedes |
| Chanel | Porsche |
| Dolce | Prada |

What is certain is that people have very real perceptions about names. Typically, judgments are made before a person is met, such as at job interviews or in school. A survey of 3,000 teachers found that 49% of teachers make assumptions about their pupils based on their name. One in three admitted that certain names spell a troublemaker to them, including Callum, Brandon, Chelsea, and Aleisha, while the names Christopher, Edward, Rebecca, and Charlotte were assumed to belong to brighter children.

The research also indicated that there are certain names more likely to initiate strong responses in people than others. A study analyzed the number of stickers given to children as rewards for good behavior. Children named Abigail and Jacob are more likely to be praised for being well behaved than children named Beth and Josh, and children who do not shorten their name or go by nicknames are more likely to be better behaved, too.

Even more research suggests girls who are given particularly "girly" names—think Tiana, Kayla, and Isabella—are much more likely to misbehave when they reach school age, and it's even more of a problem when there's more than one child in the classroom with the same name. Poor Isabella. These "feminine" girls were also far less likely to choose subjects at school like math and science, while their sisters with more masculine names—such as Morgan, Alexis, and Ashley—were encouraged to excel in these courses.

Personality and character have a far greater influence than name alone and after a while, a name becomes just a name.

## Ivy League names

| | |
|---|---|
| Alcott | Graydon |
| Arthur | Katherine |
| Beatrice | Martha |
| Caroline | Robert |
| Charles | Victoria |

## Names which sound "clever"

| | |
|---|---|
| Abner | Shanahan |
| Cassidy | Todd |
| Haley | Ulysses |
| Penelope | Washington |
| Portia | Wylie |

# Quirky names

There are lots of advantages to having a quirky name. For one thing, your child's name will never be forgotten by other people, and if they do something influential with their life their name could become an inspiration for other parents. On the other hand, a quirky name often requires a quirky personality. If you don't think your genes could stand up to a name like Satchel or Kerensa, perhaps it's time to think of one a little more run-of-the-mill.

A quirky name often says more about the parents than the child, whose own personalities may affect the personality of their child in a significant way. A conventional family who names their baby John will probably find he becomes a conventional child, whereas a quirky family who names their baby Zanzibar will also find he develops a quirky personality. The name itself is not the leading factor; it's the quirky or conventional behavior encouraged by the parents who chose the name that is.

Children who are told they have inherited an ancestor's name or are named after an influential character from history seem to be more driven and focused than children who are told disappointingly, "We just liked the sound of it." As a parent, therefore, it seems it's okay to pick an unusual name if you have a story or reason behind it. So naming your child Atticus (after Atticus Finch from Harper Lee's *To Kill A Mockingbird*, known for being a strong and moral character), or even Harper (like the Beckhams did recently), may not be a bad idea . . .

However, be warned: there is also new research from baby website Bounty, which says as many as one in five parents regrets their choice of baby name. Of the 3,000 parents interviewed, 20% said they no longer thought the unusual choice of spelling or pronunciation was appropriate. Around 8% said they were tired of people mispronouncing their child's name, and 10% thought the novelty of the original pick had worn off. They also said they would now pick a new name which had not occurred to them or been an option before.

## What not to call your child . . .

In Pennsylvania a few years ago there was a case of a supermarket bakery refusing to ice the words "Happy Birthday, Adolf Hitler" onto a three-year-old's birthday cake. The parents were able to eventually fulfill the order at another shop, but as a result of the publicity surrounding the event CPS were called in to assess the child's home and Adolf, along with his siblings JoyceLynn Aryan Nation, and Honszlynn Hinler Jeannie, were taken into care.

## Controversial names adopted by real people

Adolf Hitler
Beelzebub
Desdemona
Hannibal Lecter

Himmler
Jezebel
Lucifer
Mussolini
Stalin
Voldemort

While avoiding any kind of possible connection to a fictional character is nigh on impossible, you can help make things easier for your child by educating them about their namesake and encouraging them to read more about them. Stay up-to-date with new cartoons and children's characters in 2013 to prepare both yourself and your child for toddlerdom and childhood. That way they can be proud of their name and have ammunition if things get rough in the schoolyard.

## Cartoon characters named after real people

Yogi Bear (named after baseball player Yogi Berra)

Alvin, Simon, and Theodore Chipmunk (named after record executives)

Garfield (named after creator Jim Davis's grandfather)

Calvin and Hobbes (named after John Calvin [theologian] and Thomas Hobbes [philosopher])

Rock Lee (from *Naruto*, named after Bruce Lee)

Jimmy Neutron (named after the scientist James Chadwick, whose nickname was Jimmy Neutron)

Oscar (from *Cerebus*, named after writer Oscar Wilde)
Homer, Marge, Lisa, and Maggie Simpson (named
after creator Matt Groening's family members)
Teenage Mutant Ninja Turtles (all named
after Renaissance painters: Raphael,
Michelangelo, Donatello, and Leonardo)

## Nicknames

Nicknames are unavoidable. They can range from the
common—Mike from Michael, Sam from Samantha—to
the trendy, funny or downright insulting.

Don't be put off though if the name you love has an
unfortunate nickname associated with it—if you don't
encourage the use of nicknames, chances are one won't
stick. Another way to avoid embarrassing nicknames is to
select one for your child that you actually like so that others
don't even get a mention. Call your daughter Elizabeth by
the name Liz, Lizzie, or Libby if you don't like Betty or Beth,
and no one will even consider the alternatives.

You can pre-empt possible nicknames to some extent by
saying the name you've chosen out loud and trying to find
rhymes for it. This is a clever way to avoid playground
chants and nursery rhyme-type insults, such as Dora the
Explorer or Georgie Porgie. But don't be too concerned
about playground chants—most children are subjected to it
at some point and emerge unscathed.

Pronunciation matters: a Swedish couple
were once banned from naming their child
"Brfxxccxxmnpcccclllmmnprxvclmnckssqlbb11116,"
which they claimed was pronounced "Albin."

# Your last name

Try to avoid first names that might lead to unfortunate
phrases when combined with your last name, to prevent a
lifetime of embarrassment for your child. The best way to
work out if this might happen is to write down all the names
you like alongside your child's last name and have someone
else read them out loud. This second pair of eyes and ears
might just spot something you didn't.

The age of the internet has given parents a wonderful new
weapon in their baby-naming arsenal: the search engine.
Before you settle on anything final, try searching for any
examples of the complete first, middle, and last name of
your new baby. You may find out that your baby has an
axe-murderer namesake—or, like one of my colleagues, the
same name as a well-known porn star.

## Unfortunate first name/last name combinations

| | |
|---|---|
| Anna Sasin | Ben Dover |
| Barb Dwyer | Duane Pipe |
| Barry Cade | Grace Land |

| | |
|---|---|
| Harry Rump | Oliver Sutton |
| Isabella Horn | Paige Turner |
| Justin Time | Russell Sprout |
| Mary Christmas | Stan Still |

There is also the danger of your child being subjected to having a Spoonerism made out of their name, where the first letters or syllables get swapped around to form new words. Named after the Reverend Dr William Archibald Spooner (1844–1930), a spoonerism can be created out of almost anything to make clever, amusing, or downright inappropriate phrases instead. An unfortunate and recent example of this would be Angelina Jolie and Brad Pitt's daughter Shiloh, whom they named Shiloh Jolie-Pitt to avoid the inevitable Shiloh Pitt spoonerism.

Twitter has recently become a hot spot for spoonerisms, with celebrites such as Justin Bieber and Nick Jonas calling each other "Bustin Jieber" and "Jick Nonas." Well, no one ever said spoonerisms have to make sense . . .

## Famous name spoonerisms

Justin Bieber (bustin jieber)
Shirley Bassey (burly chassis)
Gene Kelly (keen jelly)
Jude Law (lewd jaw)
Nick Jonas (jick nonas)
Paul Walker (wall porker)
Sarah Palin (para sailing)
Shiloh Pitt (pile o' s***)

# Initials

What last name will your baby have? Will it lend itself easily to amusing acronyms when coupled with certain first and middle names? My brother-in-law was going to be called Andrew Steven Schmitt before he was born, until his parents realized at the last minute what his initials would spell . . .

It's worth taking the time to think about how credit cards display names or seeing your child's name written out on a form. Nobody should have to go through life known as S. Lugg because their parents didn't think that far ahead.

---

## Amusing initials

Earl E. Bird

I.C. Blood

Kay F. Cee

I. P. Freely

Al E. Gador

Angie O. Graham

S. Lugg

Warren T.

H. I. Vee

Gene E. Yuss

---

## Medical terms used as names

The following list was provided by a practicing midwife, who has vivid recollections of parents thinking they were naming their children something unique and original, only to be told the name they'd chosen was a medical term.

Chlamydia (pronounced cler-mid-EE-ya)
Eczema (pronounced ex-SEE-mah)
Female (pronounced fuh-MAH-lee)
Latrine (pronounced lah-TREE-nee)
Meconium (pronounced meh-COH-nee-um)
Syphilis (pronounced see-PHIL-iss)
Testicles (pronounced TESS-tee-clees)
Urine (pronounced yer-REE-nee)
Vagina (pronounced vaj-EE-nah)

# Using family names

Some families have a strong tradition of using names for babies that come from the family tree. There are instances where naming your son Augustine VIII is simply not an option; it's a rule. Another way families do this is to give children the name of their parent of the same sex and add "Junior" (Jr.) to the end. This could potentially create a problem if that child then decides to carry on the tradition and name their child after themselves—after all, who wants to be known as Frederick Jr. Jr.?

There are pros and cons with using family names.

- **Pro:** Your child will feel part of a strong tradition, which will create a sense of security for them and help make them feel a complete member of the family.

- **Pro:** If you're having a problem selecting a name you and your partner both agree on, this is a very simple solution and will make your new child's family very happy.

- **Con:** You might not actually like the name that's being passed down. Naming your child the twelfth Thumbelina in a row might not actually hold the same attraction for you as for the generation before.

- **Con:** Another drawback could be if the cultural associations with that name have changed in your ifetime and it is no longer appropriate.

In 2011 Pope Benedict decreed all names should come from the Christian calendar. Italy promptly forbade one couple from naming their child "Venerdi," meaning "Friday," because it would open the boy up to ridicule and mockery. The parents threatened to name their next son "Mercoledi," meaning "Wednesday," in response.

One way to include a family name is to compromise. You could use the name as a middle name, or refer to your baby by a nickname instead.

Another possible solution is to use monikers—if your family is insisting your daughter be called Jade, maybe you could choose Giada instead. Or if your partner is determined the next child be called Michael after himself and it turns out to be a girl, choose Michaela in its place. In many Jewish families the tradition is to take the name of a dead relative and give it to a new baby. If this thought fills you with dread, you could opt for a possible solution a lot of families do, which is to use the first initial instead. If you're not keen on Solomon, pick Samuel; if you don't like Ruth, choose Rebecca.

## Top 10 US baby boy names

| 1900 | 1950 | 2000 |
|------|------|------|
| 1. John | 1. James | 1. Jacob |
| 2. William | 2. Robert | 2. Michael |
| 3. James | 3. John | 3. Matthew |
| 4. George | 4. Michael | 4. Joshua |
| 5. Charles | 5. David | 5. Christopher |
| 6. Robert | 6. William | 6. Nicholas |
| 7. Joseph | 7. Richard | 7. Andrew |
| 8. Frank | 8. Thomas | 8. Joseph |
| 9. Edward | 9. Charles | 9. Daniel |
| 10. Henry | 10. Gary | 10. Tyler |

## Top 10 US baby girl names

| 1900 | 1950 | 2000 |
|------|------|------|
| 1. Mary | 1. Linda | 1. Emily |
| 2. Helen | 2. Mary | 2. Hannah |
| 3. Anna | 3. Patricia | 3. Madison |
| 4. Margaret | 4. Barbara | 4. Ashley |
| 5. Ruth | 5. Susan | 5. Sarah |
| 6. Elizabeth | 6. Nancy | 6. Alexis |
| 7. Florence | 7. Deborah | 7. Samantha |
| 8. Ethel | 8. Sandra | 8. Jessica |
| 9. Frances | 9. Carol | 9. Elizabeth |
| 10. Lillian | 10. Kathleen | 10. Taylor |

# Spellings and pronunciation

Once you've finally agreed upon a name, it's time to consider how you wish it to be spelt and pronounced. Some parents love experimenting with unusual variations of traditional names, while others prefer for names to be instantly recognizable.

Try to avoid making a common name too long or too unusual in its spelling as this will be the first thing your child learns how to write. They will also have to spell it out constantly during their lifetime, as other people misspell or mispronounce their name. Substituting the odd "i" for a "y" isn't too bad, but turning the name Jonathan into Jonnaythanne doesn't do anyone any favors.

**The US has seen an increase in "text speak" spellings**

| | |
|---|---|
| An | Helin |
| Camron | Jayk |
| Conna | Lora |
| Ema | Patryk |
| Esta | Samiul |
| Flicity | Summa |
| Helin | Wilym |

A palindrome name is a name that is spelt the same backwards and forwards, as with Bob, Elle, Eve, and Hannah.

# Middle names

The use of middle names is generally acknowledged to be standard practice in North America these days. In fact, it has become fairly uncommon to name a child *without* a middle name, although the use of second and third names only become popular around the turn of the 20th century. Before then, giving a child a middle name in addition to a first and last was seen as a status symbol; it was only really used when a man married a higher-class woman and they wanted to keep the woman's maiden name as a reminder of that child's heritage. Once the fashion caught on it became very popular to give more than one middle name to children of status, but it's only been since the 1900s that it became standard for everyone. Regardless of your status, a middle name can have just as much of an impact as a first name, so your choice for your own baby should be made as carefully as their first name.

Here are some common trends in 2013 to help you choose.

- **Opposite-length names.** It has become very popular to give a child either a long first name and short middle name (e.g., Jennifer Ruth, Nicholas John) and vice versa.

- **Name from the family tree.** Honoring your ancestors is another popular trend for 2013. Parents are frequently looking back to their own lineage for interesting, unusual, or influential names. It is becoming more and more common to give a parent's first name as a middle name to newborns.

- **Unusual names.** Parents who like a quirky name but aren't quite brave enough to give it to their child as a first name are using it as a middle name.

The British teenager named Captain Fantastic Faster Than Superman Spiderman Batman Wolverine Hulk And The Flash Combined, changed his name from George Garratt in 2008. He claims to have the longest name in the world. If he does then he replaces Texan woman Rhoshandiatellyneshiaunneveshenk Koyaanisquatsiuth Williams, whose 57-letter name pales in comparison to Captain's 81.

You may have already decided what middle name to give your child due to tradition or culture, in which case the following advice may be moot. In Hispanic cultures, for example, middle names are often the mother's surname or other name to promote that matriarchal lineage. Similarly, parents who have not taken each other's surnames or are not married may choose to give their child one surname as a middle name and one as a last name so both parents are represented. Other traditions may use an old family name, passed down to each first-born son or daughter to encourage a sense of family pride and history. A decision about what middle name to pass on may have therefore already been made for you, even before your own birth.

Unique middle names are very much *en vogue* right now with celebrities. The Beckhams chose "Seven" for their daughter's middle name, and there has been much discussion in the media as to why—could it be because Beckham's jersey number was seven, or that the little girl was born during the seventh hour, on the seventh day of the week, during the seventh month? Was it because the number seven is traditionally lucky? Who knows . . .

Many people actually choose to go by their middle name instead of their forename, so it could be seen as a safety net if you're worried your child won't like their name. In fact, you probably know someone in your family or workplace that has always been known as Ed or Sam when their name is actually James Edward Jones or Felicity Samantha Taylor. It's also handy in this age of living online: if you search for John Smith or Jenny Brown you'll probably find hundreds and hundreds of results. However, if you search for John

Ashok Smith or Jenny Marina Brown, there will probably be no more than one or two.

Some famous examples of multiple middle names include British musician Brian Eno, whose full name is actually Brian Peter George St. John le Baptiste de la Salle Eno, and Canadian actor Kiefer Sutherland, who has shortened his name considerably from Kiefer William Frederick Dempsey George Rufus Sutherland. Even the British Royal Family likes to give many middle names: Prince Charles's full name is Charles Philip Arthur George Mountbatten-Windsor, and Prince William is William Arthur Philip Louis Mountbatten-Windsor.

## Celebrities who go by middle names

Antonio Banderas (José Antonio Dominguez Banderas)

Bob Marley (Nesta Robert Marley)

Dakota Fanning (Hannah Dakota Fanning)

Will Ferrell (John William Ferrell)

Kelsey Grammar (Allen Kelsey Grammar)

Ashton Kutcher (Christopher Ashton Kutcher)

Hugh Laurie (James Hugh Calum Laurie)

Evangeline Lilly (Nicole Evangeline Lilly)

Brad Pitt (William Bradley Pitt)

Brooke Shields (Christa Brooke Camille Shields)

Reese Witherspoon (Laura Jean Reese Witherspoon)

# Naming twins, triplets, and more

If you have discovered you are expecting multiples, congratulations! Naming multiples needn't be any different to naming a single child . . . unless you want it to be. You could stick to the same process everyone else does, by picking an individual name for each individual child. "Octomom" Nadya Suleman, chose eight different names for her octuplets, although they do all sound reasonably similar: Isaiah, Jeremiah, Jonah, Josiah, Maliah, McCai, Nariah, and Noah.

## Twin names with the same meaning

Bernard and Brian (strong)

Daphne and Laura (laurel)

Deborah and Melissa (bee)

Dorcas and Tabitha (gazelle)

Elijah and Joel (God)

Eve and Zoe (life)

Irene and Salome (peace)

Lucius and Uri (light)

Lucy and Helen (light)

Sarah and Almira (princess)

Another option is to go with a theme. Try anagrams or names in reverse, or give each child the same initials or names with the same meaning. You could even do this if you're not expecting multiples, like the Duggar family of Arkansas, who have given each of their 19 children the initial "J"—Joshua, Jana, John-David, Jill, Jessa, Jinger, Joseph, Josiah, Joy-Anna, Jedidiah, Jeremiah, Jason, James, Justin, Jackson, Johannah, Jennifer, Jordyn-Grace, and Josie. Their newest arrival was named Jubilee, although she sadly died in late 2011.

Mariah Carey and Nick Cannon chose to use names starting with the same letter when naming their twins. Before announcing the names, Nick posted a clue to the names on Twitter, "So we r bout 2 reveal the actual names and b4 we tell em 2 our friends etc. both begin w/M's!!!!" The couple then announced the arrival of Monroe and Moroccan Scott.

Of course, when's all said and done you can just stick to giving each child a name unique to them. For triplets, quads, and more this is probably an easier choice than twisting your head around three names with the same meaning, or trying to create four anagrams you like for all of your babies. Some parents do like to use a theme though, such as going down the alphabet (think Alastair, Benjamin, Christopher, and David), or doing what the famous acting Phoenix clan did and giving each child a name to do with nature: River, Rain, Joaquin (Leaf), Liberty, and Summer.

## Popular twin names in 2013

Brandon and Brian
Daniel and David
Ella and Emma
Faith and Hope
Gabriella and Isabella
Isaac and Isaiah
Jacob and Joshua
Madison and Morgan
Matthew and Michael
Taylor and Tyler

## Celebrity twin names of the past few years

Adalynn and Noah (Chris and Deanna Daughtry)
Darby and Sullivan (Patrick Dempsey and Jillian Fink)
Eddy and Nelson (Celine Dion and Rene Angelil)
Eden and Savannah (Marcia Cross and Tom Mahoney)
Hazel and Phinnaeus (Julia Roberts and Danny Moder)
Gideon and Harper (Neil Patrick Harris and David Burtka)
Jesse and Journey (Jenna Jameson and Tito Ortiz)
Max and Bob (Charlie Sheen and Brooke Mueller)
Max and Emme (Jennifer Lopez and Marc Anthony)
Vivienne Marcheline and Knox Leon (Angelina Jolie
    and Brad Pitt)
Monroe and Moroccan Scott (Mariah Carey and
    Nick Cannon)

## Names for triplets

Abel, Bela, and Elba (anagrams)

Aidan, Diana, and Nadia (anagrams)

April, May, and June (months)

Amber, Jade, and Ruby (jewels)

Amy, May, and Mya (anagrams)

Ava, Eva, and Iva (similar)

Daisy, Lily, and Rose (flowers)

Jay, Raven, and Robin (birds)

Leah, Lianne, and Liam (similar)

Olive, Violet, and Sage (colors)

River, Rain, and Summer (nature)

" Names, once they are in common use, quickly become mere sounds, their etymology being buried, like so many of the earth's marvel beneath the dust of habit. "

Salman Rushdie

# part two

# Boys' Names

# A Boys' names

## Aaron

Hebrew, meaning 'mountain of strength'.

## Abasi

Egyptian, meaning 'male'.

## Abdiel

Biblical, meaning 'servant of God'.

## Abdul

Arabic, meaning 'servant'. Often followed with a suffix indicating who Abdul is the servant of (e.g. Abdul-Basit, servant of the creator).

## Abdullah

Arabic, meaning 'servant of God'.

## Abe

Hebrew, from Abraham, meaning 'father'.

## Abel

Hebrew, meaning 'breath' or 'breathing spirit'. Associated with the Biblical son of Adam and Eve who was killed by his brother Cain.

## Abelard

German, meaning 'resolute'.

## Aberforth

Gaelic, meaning 'mouth of the river Forth'. Name of Dumbledore's brother in the Harry Potter series.

**A**

### Abner
Hebrew, meaning 'father of light'.

### Abraham
Hebrew, meaning 'exalted father'.

### Absalom
(alt. Absalon)
Hebrew, meaning 'father/ leader of peace'.

### Acacio
Greek origin, meaning 'thorny tree'. Now widely used in Spain.

### Ace
English, meaning 'number one' or 'the best'.

### Achebe
Nigerian. Last name of famous writer Chinua Achebe.

### Achilles
Greek, mythological hero of Trojan war, whose heel was his only weak spot.

### Achim
Hebrew, meaning 'God will establish' or Polish, meaning 'The Lord exalts'.

### Ackerley
Old English, meaning 'oak meadow'. Often used as last name, many similarly spelt variants.

### Adalberto
Germanic/Spanish, meaning 'nobly bright'.

### Adam
Hebrew, meaning 'man' or 'earth'. First man to walk the earth, accompanied by Eve.

### Adão
Portuguese variant of Adam, meaning 'earth'.

### Addison
Old English, meaning 'son of Adam'. Also used as a female name.

### Ade
African, meaning 'peak' or 'pinnacle'.

**A**

## Adelard

Teutonic, meaning 'brave' or 'noble'.

## Adelbert

Old German form of Albert.

## Aden

Gaelic, meaning 'fire'.

## Adin

Hebrew, meaning 'slender' or 'voluptuous'. Also Swahili, meaning 'ornamental'.

## Aditya

Sanskrit, meaning 'belonging to the sun'.

## Adlai

Hebrew, meaning 'God is just', or sometimes 'ornamental'.

## Adler

Old German, meaning 'eagle'.

## Adley

English, meaning 'son of Adam'.

## Admon

Hebrew origin, variant of Adam meaning 'earth'. Also the name of a red peony.

## Adolph
*(alt. Adolfo)*

Old German, meaning 'noble majestic wolf'. Popularity of the name plummeted after the Second World War, for obvious reasons.

## Adonis

Phoenician, meaning 'Lord'.

---

## Movie inspirations

Anakin (Star Wars)
Edward (Twilight)
Forrest (*Forrest Gump*)
Harry (Harry Potter)
Indiana (*Raiders of the Lost Ark*)
Inigo (*The Princess Bride*)
Korben (*The Fifth Element*)
Marty (*Back to the Future*)
Red (*The Shawshank Redemption*)
Vito (*The Godfather*)

---

**A**

### Adrian

Latin origin, meaning 'from Hadria', a town in northern Italy.

### Adriel

Hebrew, meaning 'of God's flock'.

### Aeneas

Greek/Latin origin, meaning 'to praise'. Name of the hero who founded Rome in Virgil's *Aeneid*.

### Aeson

Greek origin, father of Jason.

### Afonso

Portuguese, meaning 'eager noble warrior'.

### Agamemnon

Greek, meaning 'leader of the assembly'. Figure in mythology, commanded the Greeks at the siege of Troy.

### Agathon

Greek, meaning 'good' or 'superior'.

### Agustin

Latin/Spanish, meaning 'venerated'.

### Ahab

Hebrew, meaning 'father's brother'. Pleasant way to address an uncle.

### Ahijah

Hebrew, meaning 'brother of God' or 'friend of God'.

### Ahmed

Arabic/Turkish, meaning 'worthy of praise'.

### Aidan

Gaelic, meaning 'little fire'.

### Aidric

Old English, meaning 'oaken'.

### Airyck

Old Norse, from Eric, meaning 'eternal ruler'.

### Ajani

African, meaning 'he fights for what he is'. Also Sanskrit, meaning 'of noble birth'.

### Ajax

Greek, meaning 'mourner of the Earth'. Another Greek hero from the siege of Troy.

### Ajay

Indian, meaning 'unconquerable'.

### Ajit

Indian, meaning 'invincible'.

### Akeem

Arabic, meaning 'wise or insightful'.

### Akio

Japanese, meaning 'bright man'.

### Akira

Japanese, meaning 'intelligent'.

### Akiva

Hebrew, meaning 'to protect' or 'to shelter'.

### Akon

American, made popular by the famous rapper charting in 2008/2009.

### Aksel

Hebrew/Danish, meaning 'father of peace'.

### Aladdin

Arabic, meaning 'servant of Allah'. Popular Disney character.

### Alan

*(alt. Allan, Allen, Allyn, Alun)*

Gaelic, meaning 'rock'.

### Alaric

Old German, meaning 'noble regal ruler'.

### Alastair

*(alt. Alasdair, Allister)*

Greek/Gaelic, meaning 'defending men'.

### Alban

Latin, meaning 'from Alba'. Also the Welsh and Scottish Gaelic word for 'Scotland'.

### Alberic

Germanic, meaning 'Elfin king'.

### Albert

Old German, meaning 'noble, bright, famous'.

**A**

### Albin

Latin, meaning 'white'.

### Albus

Latin, variant of Albin meaning 'white'. Also the first name of Albus Dumbledore, headmaster of Hogwarts School in the Harry Potter series.

### Alcaeus

Greek, meaning 'strength'.

### Alden

Old English, meaning 'old friend'.

### Aldis

English, meaning 'from the old house'.

### Aldo

Italian origin, meaning 'old' or 'elder'.

### Aldric

English, meaning 'old King'.

### Alec

*(alt. Alek)*

English, meaning 'defending men'.

### Aled

Welsh, meaning 'child' or 'offspring'.

### Alejandro

Spanish, meaning 'defender'. Made popular by Lady Gaga.

### Aleph

Hebrew, meaning 'first letter of the alphabet', or 'leader'.

### Alessio

Italian, meaning 'defender'.

### Alexander

*(alt. Alex, Alexandro, Alessandro, Alejandro)*

Greek, meaning 'defending men'.

### Alexei

Russian, meaning 'defender'.

### Alfonso

Germanic/Spanish, meaning 'noble and prompt, ready to struggle'.

### Alford

Old English, meaning 'old river/ford'.

### Alfred

*(alt. Alf, Alfi, Alfredo)*

English, meaning 'elf' or 'magical counsel'.

### Algernon

French, meaning 'with a moustache'.

### Ali

*(alt. Allie)*

Arabic, meaning 'noble, sublime'.

### Alijah

Hebrew, meaning 'the Lord is my God'.

### Allison

English, meaning 'noble'.

### Alois

German, meaning 'famous warrior'.

### Alok

Indian, meaning 'cry of triumph'.

### Alon

Jewish, meaning 'oak tree'.

### Alonso

*(alt. Alonzo)*

Germanic, meaning 'noble and ready'.

### Aloysius

Italian saint's name, meaning 'fame and war'.

### Alpha

First letter of the Greek alphabet.

### Alphaeus

Hebrew, meaning 'changing'.

### Alpin

Gaelic, meaning 'related to the Alps'.

### Altair

Arabic, meaning 'flying' or 'bird'.

### Alter

Yiddish, meaning 'old man'.

### Alton

Old English, meaning 'old town'.

### Alva

Latin, meaning 'white'.

### Alvie

German, meaning 'army of elves'.

**A**

### Alvin

English, meaning 'friend of elves'.

### Alwyn

Welsh, meaning 'wise friend'. May also come from the River Alwen in Wales.

### Amachi

African, meaning 'who knows what God has brought us through this child'.

### Amadeus

Latin, meaning 'God's love'.

### Amadi

African, meaning 'appeared destined to die at birth'.

### Amado

Spanish, meaning 'God's love'.

### Amador

Spanish, meaning 'one who loves'.

### Amari

Hebrew, meaning 'given by God'.

### Amarion

Arabic, meaning 'populous, flushing'.

### Amasa

Hebrew, meaning 'burden'.

### Ambrose

Greek, meaning 'undying, immortal'.

### Americo

Germanic, meaning 'ever powerful in battle'.

### Amias

Latin, meaning 'loved'.

### Amir

Hebrew, meaning 'prince' or 'treetop'.

### Amit

Hindu, meaning 'friend'.

### Ammon

Egyptian, meaning 'the hidden one'.

### Amory

German/English, meaning 'work' and 'power'.

## Amos

Hebrew, meaning 'encumbered' or 'burdened'.

## Anacletus

Latin, meaning 'called back' or 'invoked'.

## Anakin

American, meaning 'warrior'. Made famous by Anakin Skywalker in the Star Wars films.

## Ananias

Greek/Italian, meaning 'answered by the Lord'.

## Anastasius

Latin, meaning 'resurrection'.

## Anat

Jewish, meaning 'water spring'.

## Anatole

Greek, meaning 'cynical but without malice'.

## Anders

Greek, meaning 'lion man'.

## Anderson

English, meaning 'male'.

## Andrew

*(alt. Andreas, Andre, Andy)*

Greek, meaning 'man' or 'warrior'.

## Androcles

Greek, meaning 'glory of a warrior'.

## Angel

Greek, meaning 'messenger'.

## Angelo

Italian, meaning 'angel'.

## Angus

Scottish, meaning 'one choice'.

## Anil

Sanskrit, meaning 'air' or 'wind'.

## Anselm

German, meaning 'helmet of God'.

## Anson

English, meaning 'son of Agnes'.

## Anthony

English, from the old Roman family name.

## Antipas

Israeli, meaning 'for all or against all'.

## Antwan

Old English, meaning 'flower'.

## Apollo

Greek, meaning 'to destroy'. Greek god of the sun.

## Apostolos

Greek, meaning 'apostle'.

## Ara

Armenian. Ara was a legendary king.

## Aragorn

Literary, used by Tolkien in *The Lord of the Rings* trilogy.

## Aram

Hebrew, meaning 'Royal Highness'.

## Aramis

Latin, meaning 'swordsman'.

## Arcadio

Greek/Spanish, from a place in ancient Greece. The word 'Arcadia' (meaning paradise) comes from this.

## Archibald

*(alt. Archie)*

Old German, meaning 'genuine/bold/brave'.

## Ardell

Latin, meaning 'eager/burning with enthusiasm'.

## Arden

Celtic, meaning 'high'.

## Ares

Greek, meaning 'ruin'. Son of Zeus and Greek god of war.

## Ari

Hebrew, meaning 'lion' or 'eagle'.

## Arias

Germanic, meaning 'lion'.

## Ariel

Hebrew, meaning 'lion of God'. One of the archangels, the angel of healing and new beginnings.

**Arild**

Old Norse, meaning 'battle commander'.

**Aris**

Greek, meaning 'best figure'.

**Ariston**

Greek, meaning 'the best'.

**Aristotle**

Greek, meaning 'best'.
Also a famous philosopher.

**Arjun**

Sanskrit, meaning 'white'.

**Arkady**

Greek, region of central Greece.

**Arlan**

Gaelic, meaning 'pledge' or 'oath'.

**Arlie**

Old English place name, meaning 'eagle wood'.

**Arlis**

Hebrew, meaning 'pledge'.

**Arlo**

Spanish, meaning 'barberry tree'.

**Armand**

Old German, meaning 'soldier'.

**Armani**

Same origin as Armand meaning 'soldier', nowadays closely associated with the Italian designer.

**Arnaldo**

Spanish, meaning 'eagle power'.

**Arnav**

Indian, meaning 'the sea'.

**Arnold**

Old German, meaning 'eagle ruler'.

**Arrow**

English, from the common word denoting weaponry.

**Art**

Irish, name of a warrior in Irish mythology, Art Oenfer (Art the Lonely).

**A**

### Arthur
*(alt. Artie, Artis)*
Celtic, probably from 'artos', meaning 'bear'. Made famous by the tales of King Arthur and the Knights of the Round Table.

### Arturo
Celtic or Italian, meaning 'strong as a bear'.

### Arvel
From the Welsh 'Arwel', meaning 'wept over'.

### Arvid
English, meaning 'eagle in the woods'.

### Arvind
Indian, meaning 'red lotus'.

### Arvo
Finnish, meaning 'value' or 'worth'.

### Arwen
Welsh, meaning 'fair' or 'fine'.

### Asa
Hebrew, meaning 'doctor' or 'healer'.

### Asante
African, meaning 'thank you'.

### Asher
Hebrew, meaning 'fortunate' or 'lucky'.

### Ashley
Old English, meaning 'ash meadow'.

### Ashok
Sanskrit, meaning 'not causing sorrow'.

### Ashton
English, meaning 'settlement in the ash-tree grove'.

### Aslan
Turkish, meaning 'lion'. Strongly associated with the lion from C. S. Lewis's *The Lion, The Witch, and The Wardrobe*.

### Asriel
Hebrew, meaning 'help of God'.

### Astrophel
Latin, meaning 'star lover'.

**A**

## Athanasios

Greek, meaning 'eternal life'.

## Afílio

Portuguese, meaning 'father'.

## Atlas

Greek, meaning 'to carry'. In Greek mythology Atlas was a Titan forced to carry the weight of the heavens.

## Atlee

Hebrew, meaning 'God is just'.

## Atticus

Latin, meaning 'from Athens'.

## Auberon

Old German, meaning 'royal bear'.

## Aubrey

Old German, meaning 'power'.

## Auden

Old English, meaning 'old friend'.

## Audie

Old English, meaning 'noble strength'.

## August

Latin, meaning 'magnificent'.

## Literary names

Atticus (*To Kill A Mockingbird*, Harper Lee)
Cash (*As I Lay Dying*, William Faulkner)
Gatsby (*The Great Gatsby*, F. Scott Fitzgerald)
Holden (*The Catcher in the Rye*, J. D. Salinger)
Ishmael (*Moby Dick*, Herman Melville)
Rhett (*Gone With The Wind*, Margaret Mitchell)
Santiago (*Old Man and the Sea*, Ernest Hemingway)
Uncas (*The Last of the Mohicans*, James Fenimore Cooper)
Winfield (*The Grapes of Wrath*, John Steinbeck)
Yossarian (*Catch-22*, Joseph Heller)

## Augustas
*(alt. Augustus)*
Latin, meaning 'venerated'.

## Aurelien
French, meaning 'golden'.

## Austin
Latin, meaning 'venerated'.
Also a city in Texas.

## Avi
Hebrew, meaning 'father of a multitude of nations'.

## Awnan
Irish, meaning 'little Adam'.

## Axel
Hebrew, meaning 'father is peace'. Made famous by Guns 'n' Roses frontman Axl Rose.

## Azarel
Hebrew, meaning 'helped by God'.

## Azaryah
Hebrew, meaning 'helped by God'.

## Azriel
Hebrew, meaning 'God is my help'.

## Azuko
African, meaning 'past glory'.

# B Boys' names

### Babe

American, meaning 'baby'. Associated with baseball legend 'Babe' Ruth.

### Baden

German, meaning 'battle'.

### Bailey

English, meaning 'bailiff'.

### Baird

Scottish, meaning 'poet' or 'one who sings ballads'.

### Bakari

Swahili, meaning 'hope' or 'promise'.

### Baker

English, from the word 'baker'.

### Baldwin

Old French, meaning 'bold, brave friend'.

### Balin

Old English. Balin was one of the Knights of the Round Table.

### Balthazar

Babylonian, meaning 'protect the King'.

### Balvinder

Hindu, meaning 'merciful, compassionate'.

### Bannon

Irish, meaning 'descendant of O'Banain'.

**B**

## Barack

African, meaning 'blessed'. Made popular by the 44th President of the United States Barack Obama.

## Barclay

Old English, meaning 'birch tree meadow'.

## Barker

Old English, meaning 'shepherd'.

## Barnaby

*(alt. Barney)*

Greek, meaning 'son of consolation'.

## Barnard

English, meaning 'strong as a bear'.

## Baron

Old English, meaning 'young warrior'.

## Barrett

English, meaning 'strong as a bear'.

## Barron

Old German, meaning 'old clearing'.

## Barry

Irish Gaelic, meaning 'fair haired'.

## Bart

Hebrew, from Bartholomew meaning 'son of the farmer'. Made popular by the TV character Bart Simpson.

## Barton

Old English, meaning 'barley settlement'.

## Baruch

Hebrew, meaning 'blessed'.

## Bascom

Old English, meaning 'from Bascombe'.

## Bashir

Arabic, meaning 'well-educated' and 'wise'.

## Basil

Greek, meaning 'royal, kingly'.

## Basim

Arabic, meaning 'smile'.

**B**

### Bastien
Greek, meaning 'revered'.

### Baxter
Old English, meaning 'baker'.

### Bayard
French, meaning 'auburn haired'.

### Bayo
Nigerian, meaning 'to find joy'.

### Baz
Irish Gaelic, meaning 'fair-haired'.

### Beau
French, meaning 'handsome'.

### Biblical names

David
John
Joseph
Luke
Mark
Matthew
Michael
Paul
Peter
Simon

### Beck
Old Norse, meaning 'stream'.

### Beckett
Old English, meaning 'beehive' or 'bee cottage'. Associated with the Irish writer Samuel Beckett.

### Beckham
English, meaning 'homestead by the stream'. Made famous by English soccer star David Beckham.

### Béla
Hungarian, meaning 'within'.

### Belarius
Shakespearean, meaning 'a banished lord'.

### Benedict
Latin, meaning 'blessed'.

### Benjamin
(alt. Ben)
Hebrew, meaning 'son of the south'.

### Bennett
French/Latin vernacular form of Benedict, meaning 'blessed'.

**B**

## Benoit

French form of Benedict, meaning 'blessed'.

## Benson

English, meaning 'son of Ben'.

## Bentley

Old English, meaning 'bent grass meadow'.

## Benton

Old English, meaning 'town in the bent grass'.

## Beriah

Hebrew, meaning 'in fellowship' or 'in envy'.

## Bernard

*(alt. Bernie)*

Germanic, meaning 'strong, brave bear'.

## Berry

Old English, meaning 'berry'.

## Bert

*(alt. Bertram, Bertrand)*

Old English, meaning 'illustrious'.

## Berton

Old English, meaning 'bright settlement'.

## Bevan

Welsh, meaning 'son of Evan'.

## Bicknell

Old English, meaning 'from Bicknell'.

## Bilal

Arabic, meaning 'wetting, refreshing'.

## Bill

*(alt. Billy)*

English, from William, meaning 'determined' or 'resolute'.

## Birch

Old English, meaning 'bright' or 'shining'.

## Birger

Norwegian, meaning 'rescue'.

## Bishop

Old English, meaning 'bishop'.

## Bjorn

Old Norse, meaning 'bear'.

## Bladen

Hebrew, meaning 'hero'.

## Blaine

Irish Gaelic, meaning 'yellow'.

## Blair

English, meaning 'plain'.

## Blaise

French, meaning 'lisp' or 'stutter'.

## Blake

Old English, meaning 'dark, black'.

## Blas

*(alt. Blaze)*

German, meaning 'firebrand'.

## Bo

Scandinavian, short form of Robert, meaning 'bright fame'.

## Boaz

Hebrew, meaning 'swiftness' or 'strength'.

## Bob

*(alt. Bobby)*

Old German, from Robert, meaning 'bright fame'.

## Boden

*(alt. Bodie)*

Scandinavian, meaning 'shelter'.

## Bogumil

Slavic, meaning 'God's favor'.

## Bond

Old English, meaning 'peasant farmer'.

## Boris

Slavic, meaning 'battle glory'.

## Bosten

English, meaning 'town by the woods'.

## Bowen

Welsh, meaning 'son of Owen'.

## Boyd

Scottish Gaelic, meaning 'yellow'.

## Brad

*(alt. Bradley)*

Old English, meaning 'broad' or 'wide'.

**B**

**B**

## Saints' names

Anselm
Bartholomew
Francis
Gabriel
Gregory
Jerome
Nicholas
Philip
Stephen
Thomas

### Brady
Irish, meaning 'large-chested'.

### Bradyn
*(alt. Braden, Bradan)*
Gaelic, meaning 'descendant of Bradan'.

### Bram
Gaelic, meaning 'raven'.

### Brando
Old Norse, meaning 'sword' or 'flaming torch'. Associated with movie star Marlon Brando.

### Brandon
Old English, meaning 'gorse'.

### Brandt
Old English, meaning 'beacon'.

### Brannon
Gaelic, meaning 'raven'.

### Branson
English, meaning 'son of Brand'.

### Brant
Old English, meaning 'hill'.

### Braulio
Greek, meaning 'shining'.

### Brendan
Gaelic, meaning 'prince'.

### Brennan
Gaelic, meaning 'teardrop'.

### Brenton
English, from Brent, meaning 'hill'.

### Brett
English, meaning 'a Breton'.

**B**

### Brian

Gaelic, meaning 'high' or 'noble'.

### Brice

Latin, meaning 'speckled'.

### Brier

French, meaning 'heather'.

### Brock

Old English, meaning 'badger'.

### Broderick

English, meaning 'ruler'.

### Brody

Gaelic, meaning both 'ditch' and 'brother'.

### Brogan

Irish, meaning 'sturdy shoe'.

### Bronwyn

Welsh, meaning 'white breasted'.

### Brook

English, meaning 'stream'.

### Bruce

Scottish, meaning 'high' or 'noble'.

### Bruno

Germanic, meaning 'brown'.

### Bryant

English variant of Brian, meaning 'high' or 'noble'.

### Bryce

Scottish, meaning 'of Britain'.

### Brycen

Scottish, meaning 'son of Bryce'.

### Bryden

Irish, meaning 'strong one'.

### Bryson

Welsh, meaning 'descendant of Brice'.

### Bubba

American, meaning 'boy'.

### Buck

American, meaning 'goat' or 'deer'.

**B**

## Bud
*(alt. Buddy)*
American, meaning 'friend'.

## Burdett
Middle English, meaning 'bird'.

## Burke
French, meaning 'fortified settlement'.

## Burl
French, meaning 'knotty wood'.

## Buzz
American, shortened form of Busby, meaning 'village in the thicket'. Associated with the astronaut Buzz Aldrin.

## Byron
Old English, meaning 'barn'. Made famous by the poet Lord Byron.

# C Boys' names

## Cabot
Old English, meaning 'to sail'.

## Cade
(alt. Caden)
English, meaning 'round, lumpy'.

## Cadence
Latin, meaning 'with rhythm'.

## Cadogan
Welsh, meaning 'battle glory and honor'.

## Caedmon
Celtic, meaning 'wise warrior'.

## Caelan
Gaelic, meaning 'slender'.

## Caerwyn
(alt. Carwyn, Gerwyn)
Welsh, meaning 'white fort' or 'settlement'.

## Caesar
(alt. Cesar)
Latin, meaning 'head of hair'. Made famous by the first Roman emperor Julius Caesar.

## Caetano
Portuguese, meaning 'from Gaeta, Italy'

## Caiden
Arabic, meaning 'companion'.

## Caillou
French, meaning 'pebble'.

# C

### Cain
Hebrew, meaning 'full of beauty'.

### Cainan
Hebrew, meaning 'possessor' or 'purchaser'.

### Cairo
Egyptian city.

### Cal
Short form of names beginning Cal-.

### Calder
Scottish, meaning 'rough waters'.

### Caleb
Hebrew, meaning 'dog'.

### Calen
From Caleb, meaning 'dog'.

### Calix
Greek, meaning 'very handsome'.

### Callahan
Irish, meaning 'contention' or 'strife'.

### Callum
Gaelic, meaning 'dove'.

### Calvin
French, meaning 'little bald one'.

### Camden
Gaelic, meaning 'winding valley'.

### Cameron
Scottish Gaelic, meaning 'crooked nose'.

### Camillo
Latin, meaning 'free born' or 'noble'.

### Campbell
Scottish Gaelic, meaning 'crooked mouth'.

### Canaan
Hebrew, meaning 'to be humbled'.

### Candido
Latin, meaning 'candid' or 'honest'.

**C**

## Cannon

French, meaning 'of the church'.

## Canton

French, meaning 'dweller of corner'. Also name given to areas of Switzerland.

## Cappy

Italian, meaning 'lucky'.

## Carden

Old English, meaning 'wool carder'.

## Carey

Gaelic, meaning 'love'.

## Carl

Old Norse, meaning 'free man'.

## Carlo

Italian form of Carl, meaning 'free man'.

## Carlos

Spanish form of Carl, meaning 'free man'.

## Carlton

Old English, meaning 'free peasant settlement'.

## Carmelo

Latin, meaning 'garden' or 'orchard'.

## Carmen

Latin/Spanish, meaning 'song'.

## Carmine

Latin, meaning 'song'.

## Carnell

English, meaning 'defender of the castle'.

## Carson

*(alt. Carsten)*

Scottish, meaning 'marsh-dwellers'.

## Carter

Old English, meaning 'transporter of goods'.

## Cary

Old Celtic river name. Also means 'love'.

## Case

*(alt. Casey)*

Irish Gaelic, meaning 'alert' or 'watchful'.

# C

### Cash

Latin, shortened form of Cassius, meaning 'empty, hollow'.

### Casimer

Slavic, meaning 'famous destroyer of peace'.

### Cason

Latin, from Cassius, meaning 'empty' or 'hollow'.

### Casper

Persian, meaning 'treasurer'.

### Caspian

English, meaning 'of the Caspy people'. From the Caspian Sea.

### Cassidy

Gaelic, meaning 'curly haired'.

### Cassius

*(alt. Cassio)*

Latin, meaning 'empty, hollow'.

### Cathal

Celtic, meaning 'battle rule'.

### Cato

Latin, meaning 'all-knowing'.

### Cecil

Latin, meaning 'blind'.

### Cedar

English, name of an evergreen tree.

## TV personality names

Billy (Bush)
Conon (O'Brien)
Jay (Leno)
Jeff (Probst)
Jon (Stewart)

Mario (Lopez)
Nick (Cannon)
Ryan (Seacrest)
Stephen (Colbert)
Tom (Bergeron)

**C**

## Cedric

Welsh, meaning 'spectacular bounty'.

## Celestino

Spanish/Italian meaning 'heavenly'.

## Chad

(alt. Chadrick)

Old English, meaning 'warlike, warrior'.

## Chaim

Hebrew, meaning 'life'.

## Champion

English, from the word 'champion'.

## Chance

English, from the word 'chance, meaning 'good fortune'.

## Chandler

Old English, meaning 'candle maker and seller'.

## Charles

(alt. Charlie)

Old German, meaning 'free man'.

## Chase

Old French, meaning 'huntermen'.

## Chaska

Native American name usually given to first son.

## Che

Spanish, shortened form of José. Made famous by Che Guevara.

## Chesley

Old English, meaning 'camp on the meadow'.

## Chester

Latin, meaning 'camp of soldiers'.

## Chima

Old English, meaning 'hilly land'.

## Christian

English, from the word 'Christian'.

## Christophe

French variant of Christopher, meaning 'bearing Christ inside'.

# C

## Christopher
Greek, meaning 'bearing Christ inside'.

## Cian
Irish, meaning 'ancient'.

## Ciaran
Irish, meaning 'black'.

## Cicero
Latin, meaning 'chickpea'. Also a famous Roman philosopher and orator.

## Cimarron
City in western Kansas.

## Ciprian
Latin, meaning 'from Cyprus'.

## Ciro
Spanish, meaning 'sun'.

## Clancy
Old Irish, meaning 'red warrior'.

## Clarence
Latin, meaning 'one who lives near the river Clare'.

## Clark
Latin, meaning 'clerk'.

## Claude
(alt. Claudie, Claudio, Claudius)
Latin, meaning 'lame'.

## Claus
Variant of Nicholas, meaning 'people of victory'.

## Clay
English, from the word 'clay'.

## Clement
(alt. Clem)
Latin, meaning 'merciful'.

## Cleo
Greek, meaning 'glory'.

## Cletus
Greek, meaning 'illustrious'.

## Cliff
(alt. Clifford, Clifton)
English, from the word 'cliff'.

## Clint
(alt. Clinton)
Old English, meaning 'fenced settlement'.

## Clive

Old English, meaning 'cliff' or 'slope'.

## Clyde

Scottish, from the river in Glasgow.

## Coby

*(alt. Cody, Colby)*

Irish, son of Oda.

## Colden

Old English, meaning 'dark valley'.

## Cole

Old French, meaning 'coal black'.

## Coley

Old English, meaning 'coal black'.

## Colin

Gaelic, meaning 'young creature'.

## Colson

Old English, meaning 'coal black'.

## Colton

English, meaning 'swarthy'.

## Columbus

Latin, meaning 'dove'.

## Colwyn

Welsh, from the river in Wales.

## Conan

Gaelic, meaning 'wolf'.

## Conley

Gaelic, meaning 'sensible'.

## Connell

*(alt. Connolly)*

Irish, meaning 'high' or 'mighty'.

## Connor

*(alt. Conrad, Conroy)*

Irish, meaning 'lover of hounds'.

## Constant

*(alt. Constantine)*

English, from the word 'constant'.

## Cooper

Old English, meaning 'barrel maker'.

**C**

# C

### Corban

Hebrew, meaning 'dedicated and belonging to God'.

### Corbett
*(alt. Corbin, Corby)*

Norman French, meaning 'young crow'.

### Cordell

Old English, meaning 'cord maker'.

### Corey

Gaelic, meaning 'hill hollow'.

---

## Uncommon three syllable names

Alastair
Barnaby
Dominic
Elijah
Elliot
Gideon
Nathaniel
Reginald
Theodore

---

### Corin

Latin, meaning 'spear'.

### Cormac

Gaelic, meaning 'impure son'.

### Cornelius
*(alt. Cornell)*

Latin, meaning 'horn'.

### Cortez

Spanish, meaning 'courteous'.

### Corwin

Old English, meaning 'heart's friend' or 'companion'.

### Cosimo
*(alt. Cosme, Cosmo)*

Italian, meaning 'order' or 'beauty'.

### Coty

French, meaning 'riverbank'.

### Coulter

English, meaning 'young horse'.

### Courtney

Old English, meaning 'domain of Curtis'.

### Covey

English, meaning 'flock of birds'.

**C**

## Cowan
Gaelic, meaning 'hollow in the hill'.

## Craig
Welsh, meaning 'rock'.

## Crispin
Latin, meaning 'curly haired'.

## Croix
French, meaning 'cross'.

## Cruz
Spanish, meaning 'cross'.

## Curran
Gaelic, meaning 'dagger' or 'hero'.

## Curtis
*(alt. Curt)*
Old French, meaning 'courteous'.

## Cutler
Old English, meaning 'knife maker'.

## Cyprian
English, meaning 'from Cyprus'.

## Cyril
Greek, meaning 'master' or 'Lord'.

## Cyrus
Persian, meaning 'Lord'.

---

## Popular American names for boys and girls

| | |
|---|---|
| Aubree | Kendra |
| Brayden | Lacey |
| Cooper | Landon |
| Grayson | Misty |
| Kayla | Peyton |

## C

### Popular names of English and Scottish Kings and Consorts

| | |
|---|---|
| Alexander | James |
| Charles | Richard |
| Edward | Robert |
| George | Stephen |
| Henry | William |

# D

## Boys' names

### Dafydd

Welsh, meaning 'beloved'.

### Daichi

Japanese, meaning 'great wisdom'.

### Daisuke

Japanese, meaning 'lionhearted'.

### Dakari

African, meaning 'happy'.

### Dakota

Native American, meaning 'friend' or 'ally'.

### Dale

Old English, meaning 'valley'.

### Dallin

English, meaning 'dweller in the valley'.

### Dalton

English, meaning 'town in the valley'.

### Daly

Gaelic, meaning 'assembly'.

### Damarion

Greek, meaning 'gentle'.

### Damian

(alt. Damon)

Greek, meaning 'to tame, subdue'.

# D

## Dane
Old English, meaning 'from Denmark'.

## Daniel
(alt. Dan, Danny)
Hebrew, meaning 'God is my judge'.

## Dante
Latin, meaning 'lasting'. Associated with the famous Italian 13th century poet Dante Alighieri.

## Darby
Irish, meaning 'without envy'.

## Darcy
Gaelic, meaning 'dark'. Associated with Jane Austen's Mr Darcy.

## Dario
(alt. Darius)
Greek, meaning 'Kingly'.

## Darnell
Old English, meaning 'the hidden spot'.

## Darragh
Irish, meaning 'dark oak'.

## Darrell
(alt. Daryl)
Old English, meaning 'open'.

## Darren
(alt. Darrian)
Gaelic, meaning 'great'.

## Darrick
Old German, meaning 'power of the tribe'.

## Darshan
Hindi, meaning 'vision'.

## Darwin
Old English, meaning 'dear friend'.

## Dash
(alt. Dashawn)
American, meaning 'enlightened one'.

## Dashiell
French, meaning 'page boy'.

## David
(alt. Dave, Davey, Davie, Davian)
Hebrew, meaning 'beloved'.

**D**

## Davis

Old English, meaning 'son of David'.

## Dawson

Old English, meaning 'son of David'.

## Dax

*(alt. Daxton)*

French, from the town in southwestern France.

## Dayal

Indian, meaning 'kind'.

## Dayton

Old English, meaning 'David's place'.

## Dean

Old English, meaning 'valley'.

## Declan

Irish, meaning 'full of goodness'.

## Dedric

Old English, meaning 'gifted ruler'.

## Deegan

*(alt. Deagon, Daegan)*

Irish, meaning 'black-haired'.

## Deepak

*(alt. Deepan)*

Indian, meaning 'illumination'.

## Del

*(alt. Delano, Delbert, Dell)*

Old English, meaning 'bright shining one'.

## Demetrius

Greek, meaning 'harvest lover'.

## Dempsey

Irish, meaning 'proud'.

## Denham

*(alt. Denholm)*

Old English, meaning 'valley settlement'.

## Dennis

*(alt. Denny, Denton)*

English, meaning 'follower of Dionysius'.

## Denver

Old English, meaning 'green valley'. City in Colorado.

# D

## Old name, new fashion?

Augustus
Bertrand
Edgar
Felix
Gilbert
Hector
Jasper
Norris
Percival
Reginald
Sebastian
Theodore
Winston

### Denzil

English, meaning 'fort'. Also a town in Cornwall, England.

### Deon

Greek, meaning 'of Zeus'.

### Derek

English, meaning 'power of the tribe'.

### Dermot

Irish, meaning 'free man'.

### Desmond

Irish, meaning 'from south Munster'.

### Destin

French, meaning 'destiny'.

### Devyn

Irish, meaning 'poet'.

### Dewey

Welsh, from Dewi (David).

### Dexter

(alt. Dex)

Latin, meaning 'right-handed'.

### Dick

(alt. Dickie, Dickon)

From Richard, meaning 'powerful leader'.

### Didier

French, meaning 'much desired'.

### Diego

Spanish, meaning 'supplanter'.

### Dietrich

Old German, meaning 'power of the tribe'.

## Diggory
English, meaning 'dyke'.

## Dilbert
English, meaning 'day-bright'.

## Dimitri
*(alt. Dimitrios, Dimitris)*
Greek, meaning 'prince'.

## Dino
Diminutive of Dean, meaning 'valley'.

## Dion
Greek, short form of Dionysius.

## Dirk
Variant of Derek, meaning 'power of the tribe'.

## Dobbin
Diminutive of Robert, meaning 'bright fame'.

## Dominic
Latin, meaning 'Lord'.

## Donald
*(alt. Don, Donal, Donaldo)*
Gaelic, meaning 'great chief'.

## Donato
Italian, meaning 'gift'.

## Donnell
*(alt. Donnie, Donny)*
Gaelic, meaning 'world fighter'.

## Donovan
Gaelic, meaning 'dark-haired chief'.

## Doran
Gaelic, meaning 'exile'.

## Dorian
Greek, meaning 'descendant of Doris'.

## Douglas
*(alt. Dougal, Dougie)*
Scottish, meaning 'black river'.

## Draco
Latin, meaning 'dragon'. Made popular by the character Draco Malfoy in the Harry Potter series.

## Drake
Greek, meaning 'dragon'.

# D

## Drew
Shortened form of Andrew, Greek, meaning 'man' or 'warrior'.

## Dudley
Old English, meaning 'people's field'.

## Duff
Gaelic, meaning 'swarthy'.

## Duke
Latin, meaning 'leader'.

## Duncan
Scottish, meaning 'dark warrior'.

## Dustin
*(alt. Dusty)*
French, meaning 'brave warrior'.

## Dwayne
Irish Gaelic, meaning 'swarthy'.

## Dwight
Flemish, meaning 'blond'.

## Dwyer
Gaelic, meaning 'dark wise one'.

## Dylan
*(alt. Dillon)*
Welsh, meaning 'son of the sea'.

# E Boys' names

### Eamon
*(alt. Eames)*

Irish, meaning 'wealthy protector'.

### Earl
*(alt. Earle, Errol)*

English, meaning 'nobleman, warrior'.

### Ebb

Shortened form of Ebenezer, meaning 'stone of help'.

### Ebenezer

Hebrew, meaning 'stone of help'.

### Ed
*(alt. Edd, Eddie, Eddy)*

Shortened form of Edward, Old English, meaning 'wealthy guard'.

### Edgar
*(alt. Elgar)*

Old English, meaning 'wealthy spear'.

### Edison

English, meaning 'son of Edward'.

### Edmund

English, meaning 'wealthy protector'.

### Edric

Old English, meaning 'rich and powerful'.

### Edsel

Old German, meaning 'noble'.

## E

### Edward
(alt. Eduardo)

Old English, meaning 'wealthy guard'.

### Edwin
English, meaning 'wealthy friend'.

### Efrain
Hebrew, meaning 'fruitful'.

### Egan
Irish, meaning 'fire'.

### Einar
Old Norse, meaning 'battle leader'.

### Eladio
Greek, meaning 'Greek'.

### Elam
Hebrew, meaning 'eternal'.

### Elbert
Old English, meaning 'famous'.

### Eldon
Old English, meaning 'Ella's hill'.

### Eldred
(alt. Eldridge)

Old English, meaning 'old venerable counsel'.

### Elgin
Old English, meaning 'high minded'.

### Eli
(alt. Eliah)

Hebrew, meaning 'high'.

### Elias
(alt. Elijah)

Hebrew, meaning 'the Lord is my God'.

### Elio
Spanish, meaning 'the Lord is my God'.

### Ellery
Old English, meaning 'elder tree'.

### Elliott
Variant of Elio, Spanish, meaning 'the Lord is my God'.

### Ellis
Welsh variant of Elio, Spanish, meaning 'the Lord is my God'.

**E**

## Ellison
English, meaning 'son of Ellis'.

## Elmer
*(alt. Elmo)*
Old English, meaning 'noble';
Arabic, meaning 'aristocratic'.

## Elon
Hebrew, meaning 'oak tree'.

## Elroy
French, meaning 'king'.

## Elton
Old English, meaning 'Ella's
town'.

## Elvin
English, meaning 'elf-like'.

## Elvis
Figure in Norse mythology.
Made famous by the singer
Elvis Presley.

## Emanuel
Hebrew, meaning 'God is
with us'.

## Emeric
German, meaning 'work rule'.

## Emile
*(alt. Emiliano, Emilio)*
Latin, meaning 'eager'.

## Emlyn
Welsh, name of town in West
Wales, UK.

## Emmett
English, meaning
'universal'.

## Emrys
Welsh, meaning 'immortal'.

## Enoch
Hebrew, meaning 'dedicated'.

## Enrico
*(alt. Enrique)*
Italian form of Henry, meaning
'home ruler'.

## Enzo
Italian, short for Lorenzo,
meaning 'laurel'.

## Eoghan
*(alt. Eoin)*
Irish form of Owen, meaning
'well born' or 'noble'.

# E

### Ephron
*(alt. Effron)*
Hebrew, meaning 'dust'.

### Erasmo
*(alt. Erasmus)*
Greek, meaning 'to love'.

### Eric
Old Norse, meaning 'ruler'.

### Ernest
*(alt. Ernesto, Ernie, Ernst)*
Old German, meaning 'serious'.

### Erskine
Scottish, meaning 'high cliff'.

### Erwin
Old English, meaning 'boar friend'.

### Ethan
*(alt. Etienne)*
Hebrew, meaning 'long lived'.

### Eugene
Greek, meaning 'well born'.

### Evan
Welsh, meaning 'God is good'.

### Everard
Old English, meaning 'strong boar'.

### Everett
English, meaning 'strong boar'.

### Ewald
*(alt. Ewan, Ewell)*
Old English, from Owen, meaning 'well born' or 'noble'.

### Exton
English, meaning 'on the river Exe'.

### Ezra
Hebrew, meaning 'helper'.

# F Boys' names

**Fabian**
*(alt. Fabien, Fabio)*
Latin, meaning 'one who grows beans'.

**Fabrice**
*(alt. Fabrizio)*
Latin, meaning 'works with his hands'.

**Faisal**
Arabic, meaning 'resolute'.

**Faron**
Spanish, meaning 'pharaoh'.

**Farrell**
Gaelic, meaning 'hero'.

**Faulkner**
Latin, from 'falcon'.

**Faustino**
Latin, meaning 'fortunate'.

**Felipe**
*(alt. Filippo)*
Spanish, meaning 'lover of horses'.

**Felix**
*(alt. Felice)*
Italian/Latin, meaning 'happy'.

**Fennel**
Latin, name of a herb.

**F**

## Names of poets

Alfred (Lord Tennyson)
Allen (Ginsberg)
Dylan (Thomas)
Geoffrey (Chaucer)
Langston (Hughes)

Ralph (Waldo Emerson)
Robert (Burns)
Seamus (Heaney)
Walt (Whitman)
William (Wordsworth)

### Ferdinand
*(alt. Fernando)*
Old German, meaning 'bold voyager'.

### Fergus
*(alt. Ferguson)*
Gaelic, meaning 'supreme man'.

### Ferris
Gaelic, meaning 'rock'.

### Fidel
Latin, meaning 'faithful'.

### Finbar
Gaelic, meaning 'fair head'.

### Finian
Gaelic, meaning 'fair'.

### Finlay
*(alt. Finley, Finn)*
Gaelic, meaning 'fair-haired courageous one'.

### Finnegan
Gaelic, meaning 'fair'.

### Fintan
Gaelic, meaning 'little fair one'.

### Flavio
Latin, meaning 'yellow hair'.

**F**

## Florencio
*(alt. Florentino)*
Latin, meaning 'from Florence'.

## Florian
*(alt. Florin)*
Slavic/Latin, meaning 'flower'.

## Floyd
Welsh, meaning 'gray haired'.

## Flynn
Gaelic, meaning 'with a ruddy complexion'.

## Fortunato
Italian, meaning 'lucky'.

## Forrest
*(alt. Forest)*
Old French, meaning 'woodsman'. Made popular by the movie *Forrest Gump*.

## Foster
Old English, meaning 'woodsman'.

## Fotini
*(alt. Fotis)*
Greek, meaning 'light'.

## Francesco
*(alt. Francis, Francisco, Franco, François)*
Latin, meaning 'from France'.

## Frank
*(alt. Frankie, Franklin, Franz)*
Middle English, meaning 'free landholder'.

## Fraser
Scottish, meaning 'of the forest men'.

## Fred
*(alt. Freddie, Frederick)*
Old German, meaning 'peaceful ruler'.

## Furman
Old German, meaning 'ferryman'.

## Popular African names for boys and girls

| | |
|---|---|
| Abiba | Jelani |
| Chike | Kanene |
| Ebere | Keisha |
| Faizah | Razi |
| Fola | Salim |

# G Boys' names

### Gabe

Hebrew, shortened form of Gabriel, meaning 'hero of God'.

### Gabino

Latin, meaning 'God is my strength'.

### Gabriel

Hebrew, meaning 'hero of God'.

### Gael

English, old reference to the Celts.

### Gage
*(alt. Gaige)*

Old French, meaning 'pledge'.

### Galen

Greek, meaning 'healer'.

### Galileo

Italian, meaning 'from Galilee'.

### Ganesh

Hindi, meaning 'Lord of the throngs'. One of the Hindu deities.

### Gannon

Irish, meaning 'fair skinned'.

### Gareth
*(alt. Garth)*

Welsh, meaning 'gentle'.

### Garfield

Old English, meaning 'spear field'. Also the name of the cartoon cat.

# G

## Garland

English, as in 'garland of flowers'.

## Garnet

English, precious stone red in color.

## Garrett

*(alt. Garet)*

Germanic, meaning 'strength of the spear'.

## Gary

*(alt. Garry, Geary)*

Old English, meaning 'spear'.

## Gaspar

*(alt. Gaspard)*

Persian, meaning 'treasurer'.

## Gaston

From the region in the south of France.

## Gavin

*(alt. Gawain)*

Scottish/Welsh, meaning 'little falcon'.

## Gene

Greek, shortened form of Eugene, meaning 'well born'.

## Gennaro

Italian, meaning 'of Janus'.

## Geoffrey

Old German, meaning 'peace'.

## George

*(alt. Giorgio)*

Greek, meaning 'farmer'.

## Gerald

*(alt. Geraldo, Gerard, Gerardo, Gerhard)*

Old German, meaning 'spear ruler'.

## Geronimo

Italian, meaning 'sacred name'.

## Gerry

English, meaning 'independent'.

## Gert

Old German, meaning 'strong spear'.

## Gervase

Old German, meaning 'with honor'.

**G**

Giacomo
Italian, meaning 'God's son'.

Gibson
English, meaning 'son of Gilbert'.

Gideon
Hebrew, meaning 'tree cutter'.

Gilbert
*(alt. Gilberto)*
French, meaning 'bright promise'.

Giles
Greek, meaning 'small goat'.

Gino
Italian, meaning 'well born'.

Giovanni
Italian form of John, meaning 'God is gracious'.

Giulio
Italian, meaning 'youthful'.

Giuseppe
Italian form of Joseph, meaning 'Jehovah increases'.

Glen
*(alt. Glyn)*
English, from the word 'glen'.

Godfrey
German, meaning 'peace of God'.

Gordon
Gaelic, meaning 'large fortification'.

Gottlieb
German, meaning 'good love'.

Graeme
*(alt. Graham)*
English, meaning 'gravelled area'.

## Names from ancient Rome

Brutus
Caesar
Julius
Lucius
Marcus
Maximus
Nero
Rufus
Titus

115

# G

**Grant**

English, from the word 'grant'.

**Granville**

English, meaning 'gravelly town'.

**Gray**
(alt. Grey)

English, from the word 'gray'.

**Grayson**

English, meaning 'son of gray'.

**Green**

English, from the word 'green'.

**Greg**
(alt. Gregorio, Gregory, Grieg)

English, meaning 'watcher'.

**Griffin**

English, from the word 'griffin'.

**Guido**

Italian, meaning 'guide'.

**Guillaume**

French form of William, meaning 'strong protector'.

**Gulliver**

English, meaning 'glutton'.

**Gunther**

German, meaning 'warrior'.

**Gurpreet**

Indian, meaning 'love of the teacher'.

**Gustave**
(alt. Gus)

Scandinavian, meaning 'royal staff'.

**Guy**

English, from the word 'guy'.

**Gwyn**

Welsh, meaning 'white'.

# H Boys' names

## Habib
Arabic, meaning 'beloved one'.

## Haden
(alt. Haiden)
English, meaning 'hedged valley'.

## Hades
Greek, meaning 'sightless'. Name of the underworld in Greek mythology.

## Hadrian
From Hadria, a north Italian city.

## Hadwin
Old English, meaning 'friend in war'.

## Hakeem
Arabic, meaning 'wise and insightful'.

## Hal
(alt. Hale, Hallie)
English, nickname for Henry, meaning 'home ruler'.

## Hamid
Arabic, meaning 'praiseworthy'.

## Hamilton
Old English, meaning 'flat topped hill'.

## Hamish
Scottish form of James, meaning 'he who supplants'.

## Hampus

Swedish form of Homer, meaning 'pledge'.

## Hamza

Arabic, meaning 'lamb'.

## Han

(alt. *Hannes, Hans*)

Scandinavian, meaning 'the Lord is gracious'.

## Hank

German, form of Henry, meaning 'home ruler'.

## Hansel

German, meaning 'the Lord is gracious'.

## Hardy

English, meaning 'tough'.

## Harlan

English, meaning 'dweller by the boundary wood'.

## Harland

Old English, meaning 'army land'.

## Harley

Old English, meaning 'hare meadow'.

## Harmon

Old German, meaning 'soldier'.

## Harold

Scandinavian, meaning 'army ruler'.

## Harry

Old German, form of Henry, meaning 'home ruler'.

## Hart

Old English, meaning 'stag'.

## Names from ancient Greece

Aesop
Demetrius
Erasmus
Georgios
Homer
Jason
Lysandos
Nikolaos
Pyrrhus
Theodore

**H**

## Harvey
Old English, meaning 'strong and worthy'.

## Haskell
Hebrew, meaning 'intellect'.

## Hassan
Arabic, meaning 'handsome'.

## Haydn
(alt. Hayden)
Old English, meaning 'hedged valley'.

## Heart
English, from the word 'heart'.

## Heath
English, meaning 'heath' or 'moor'.

## Heathcliff
English, meaning 'cliff near a heath'. Made famous by Emily Bronte's novel *Wuthering Heights*.

## Heber
Hebrew, meaning 'partner'.

## Hector
Greek, meaning 'steadfast'.

## Henry
(alt. Henri, Hendrik, Hendrix)
Old German, meaning 'home ruler'.

## Henson
English, meaning 'son of Henry'.

## Herbert
(alt. Bert, Herb, Heriberto)
Old German, meaning 'illustrious warrior'.

## Herman
(alt. Herminio, Hermon)
Old German, meaning 'soldier'.

## Hermes
Greek, meaning 'messenger'.

## Herschel
Yiddish, meaning 'deer'.

## Hezekiah
Hebrew, meaning 'God gives strength'.

**H**

### Hideki
Japanese, meaning 'excellent trees'.

### Hideo
Japanese, meaning 'excellent name'.

### Hilario
Latin, meaning 'cheerful, happy'.

### Hilary
English, meaning 'cheerful'.

### Hillel
Hebrew, meaning 'greatly praised'.

### Hilliard
Old German, meaning 'battle guard'.

### Hilton
Old English, meaning 'hill settlement'.

### Hiram
Hebrew, meaning 'exalted brother'.

### Hiro
Spanish, meaning 'sacred name'.

### Hiroshi
Japanese, meaning 'generous'.

### Hirsch
Yiddish, meaning 'deer'.

### Hobart
English, meaning 'bright and shining intellect'.

### Hodge
English, meaning 'son of Roger'.

### Hogan
Gaelic, meaning 'youth'.

### Holden
English, meaning 'deep valley'.

### Hollis
Old English, meaning 'holly tree'.

### Homer
Greek, meaning 'pledge'.

**Honorius**

Latin, meaning 'honorable'.

**Horace**

Latin, name of the Roman poet.

**Houston**

Old English, meaning 'Hugh's town'.

**Howard**

Old English, meaning 'noble watchman'.

**Howell**

Welsh, meaning 'eminent and remarkable'.

**Hoyt**

Norse, meaning 'spirit' or 'soul'.

**Hristo**

From Christo, meaning 'follower of Christ'.

**Hubert**

German, meaning 'bright and shining intellect'.

**Hudson**

Old English, meaning 'son of Hugh'.

**Hugh**

(alt. Huw)

Old German, meaning 'soul, mind and intellect'.

**Humbert**

Old German, meaning 'famous giant'. Made famous by the paedophile protagonist of Vladimir Nabokov's Lolita.

**Humphrey**

Old German, meaning 'peaceful warrior'.

**Hunter**

English, from the word 'hunter'.

**Hurley**

Gaelic, meaning 'sea tide'.

**Huxley**

Old English, meaning 'Hugh's meadow'.

**Hyrum**

Hebrew, meaning 'exalted brother'.

## Names with positive meanings

Auden (Friend)

Basim (Smile)

Dustin (Brave)

Ervin (Beautiful)

Gene (Noble)

Jamal (Handsome)

Jay (Happy)

Lucas (Light)

Tate (Cheerful)

Tova (Good)

# I Boys' names

### Iago

Spanish, meaning 'he who supplants'.

### Ian
*(alt. Ion)*

Gaelic, variant of John, meaning 'God is gracious'.

### Ianto

Welsh, meaning 'gift of God'.

### Ibrahim

Arabic, meaning 'father of many'.

### Ichabod

Hebrew, meaning 'glory is good'.

### Ichiro

Japanese, meaning 'firstborn son'.

## Girls' names for boys (male spellings)

Casey
Darcy
Gene
Kay
Kelly
Kelsey
Madison
Nat
Sandy
Sasha

# I

**Idris**

Welsh, meaning 'fiery leader'.

**Ifan**

Welsh variant of John, meaning 'God is gracious'.

**Ignacio**

Latin, meaning 'ardent' or 'burning'.

**Ignatz**

German, meaning 'fiery'.

**Igor**

Russian, meaning 'Ing's soldier'.

**Ikaika**

Hawaiian, meaning 'strong'.

**Ike**

Hebrew, short for Isaac, meaning 'laughter'.

**Ilan**

Hebrew, meaning 'tree'.

**Ilias**

Variant of Elijah, Hebrew, meaning 'the Lord is my God'.

**Imanol**

Hebrew, meaning 'God is with us'.

**Indiana**

Latin, meaning 'from India'.

**Indigo**

English, describing a deep blue color.

**Indio**

Spanish, meaning 'indigenous people'.

**Ingo**

Danish, meaning 'meadow'.

**Inigo**

Spanish, meaning 'fiery'.

**Ioannis**

Greek, meaning 'the Lord is gracious'.

**Ira**

Hebrew, meaning 'full grown and watchful'.

**Irvin**

*(alt. Irving, Irwin)*

Gaelic, meaning 'green and fresh water'.

## Isaac
*(alt. Isaak)*

Hebrew, meaning 'laughter'.

## Isadore
*(alt. Isidore, Isidro)*

Greek, meaning 'gift of Isis'.

## Isai
*(alt. Isaiah, Isaias, Izaiah)*

Arabic, meaning 'protection and security'.

## Iser

Yiddish, meaning 'God wrestler'.

## Ishmael
*(alt. Ismael)*

Hebrew, meaning 'God listens'.

## Israel

Hebrew, meaning 'God perseveres'. Also the name of the country.

## Istvan

Hungarian variant of Stephen, meaning 'crowned'.

### Place names

Adrian
Austin
Bradley
Brooklyn
Cheyenne
Dallas
Glen
Houston
Paris
Tay

## Itai

Hebrew, meaning 'the Lord is with me'.

## Ivan

Hebrew, meaning 'God is gracious'.

## Ivanhoe

Russian origin, meaning 'God is gracious'. Also name of the novel by Walter Scott.

## Ivey

English, variant of Ivy.

**I**

**I**

### Ivo

French, from the word 'yves', meaning 'yew tree'.

### Ivor

Scandinavian, meaning 'yew'.

### Ivory

English, from the word 'ivory'.

## Long names

Alexander
Bartholomew
Christopher
Demetrius
Giovanni
Maximillian
Montgomery
Nathaniel
Sebastian
Zachariah

# J
## Boys' names

### Jabari
Swahili, meaning 'valiant'.

### Jabez
Hebrew, meaning 'borne in pain'.

### Jace
(alt. Jaece, Jase, Jayce)
Hebrew, meaning 'healer'.

### Jacek
(alt. Jacirto)
African, meaning 'hyacinth'.

### Jack
(alt. Jackie, Jacky)
From the Hebrew John, meaning 'God is gracious'.

### Jackson
(alt. Jaxon)
English, meaning 'son of Jack'.

### Jacob
(alt. Jaco, Jacobo, Jago)
Hebrew, meaning 'he who supplants'.

### Jacques
French form of Jack, meaning 'God is gracious'.

### Jaden
(alt. Jaden, Jadyn, Jaeden, Jaiden, Jaidyn, Jayden, Jaydin)
Hebrew, meaning 'Jehovah has heard'.

### Jafar
Arabic, meaning 'stream'.

# J

## Jagger

Old English, meaning 'one who cuts'.

## Jaheem

*(alt. Jaheim)*

Hebrew, meaning 'raised up'.

## Jahir

Hindi, meaning 'jewel'.

## Jaime

Variant for James, meaning 'he who supplants'. 'J'aime' is also French for 'I love'.

## Jair

*(alt. Jairo)*

Hebrew, meaning 'God enlightens'.

## Jake

Shortened form of Jacob, meaning 'he who supplants'.

## Jalen

Greek, meaning 'healer' or 'tranquil'.

## Jali

Swahili, meaning 'musician'.

## Jalon

Greek, meaning 'healer' or 'tranquil'.

## Jamaal

*(alt. Jamal)*

Arabic, meaning 'handsome'.

## Jamar

*(alt. Jamarcus, Jamari, Jamarion, Jamir)*

Modern variant of Jamaal, meaning 'handsome'.

## James

English, meaning 'he who supplants'.

## Jameson

*(alt. Jamison)*

English, meaning 'son of James'.

## Jamie

*(alt. Jamey, Jaimie)*

Nickname for James, meaning 'he who supplants'.

## Jamil

Arabic, meaning 'handsome'.

**J**

### Jamin

Hebrew, meaning 'son of the right hand'.

### Jan
(alt. Janko, János)

Slavic, from John meaning 'the Lord is gracious'.

### Janus

Latin, meaning 'gateway'. Roman god of doors, beginnings and endings.

### Japhet
(alt. Japheth)

Hebrew, meaning 'comely'.

### Short names

Al
Ben
Dai
Ed
Jay
Jon
Max
Rio
Sam
Ty

### Jaquez

French form of Jacques, meaning 'God is gracious'.

### Jared
(alt. Jarem, Jaren, Jaret, Jarod, Jarrod)

Hebrew, meaning 'descending'.

### Jarlath

Gaelic, from Iarlaith, from Saint Iarfhlaith.

### Jarom

Greek, meaning 'to raise and exalt'.

### Jarrell

Variant of Gerald, meaning 'spear ruler'.

### Jarrett

Old English, meaning 'spear-brave'.

### Jarvis

Old German, meaning 'with honor'.

**J**

## Jason
Greek, meaning 'healer'.

## Jasper
Greek, meaning 'treasure holder'.

## Javen
Arabic, meaning 'youth'.

## Javier
Spanish, meaning 'bright'.

## Jay
Latin, meaning 'jaybird'.

## Jaylan
(alt. Jaylen)
Greek, meaning 'healer'.

## Jeevan
Indian, meaning 'life'.

## Jefferson
English, meaning 'son of Jeffrey'.

## Jeffrey
(alt. Jeff)
Old German, meaning 'peace'.

## Jensen
Scandinavian, meaning 'son of Jan'.

## Jeremy
(alt. Jem)
Hebrew, meaning 'the Lord exalts'.

## Jeriah
Hebrew, meaning 'Jehovah has seen'.

## Jericho
Arabic, meaning 'city of the moon'.

## Jermaine
Latin, meaning 'brotherly'.

## Jerome
Greek, meaning 'sacred name'.

## Jerry
English, from Gerald, meaning 'spear ruler'.

## Jesse
Hebrew, meaning 'the Lord exists'.

J

## Jesus

Hebrew, meaning 'the Lord is Salvation' and the Son of God.

## Jethro

Hebrew, meaning 'eminent'.

## Jim

*(alt. Jimmy)*

From James, meaning 'he who supplants'.

## Jiri

*(alt. Jiro)*

Greek, meaning 'farmer'.

## Joachim

Hebrew, meaning 'established by God'.

## Joah

*(alt. João)*

Hebrew, meaning 'God is gracious' .

## Joaquin

Hebrew, meaning 'established by God'.

## Joe

*(alt. Joey, Johan, Johannes, Jomar)*

From Joseph, meaning 'Jehovah increases'.

## Joel

Hebrew, meaning 'Jehovah is the Lord'.

## John

Hebrew, meaning 'God is gracious'.

## Johnny

*(alt. Jon, Jonny)*

From Jonathan, meaning 'gift of God'.

## Jolyon

From Julian, meaning 'young'.

## Jonah

*(alt. Jonas)*

Hebrew, meaning 'dove'.

## Jonathan

*(alt. Johnathan, Johnathon, Jonathon, Jonty)*

Hebrew, meaning 'God is gracious'.

## J

**Jordan**
(alt. Jory, Judd)
Hebrew, meaning 'down-flowing'.

**Jorge**
From George, meaning 'farmer'.

**José**
Spanish variant of Joseph, meaning 'God increases'.

**Joseph**
(alt. Joss)
Hebrew, meaning 'God increases'.

**Josh**
Shortened form of Joshua, meaning 'Jehovah is salvation'.

**Joshua**
Hebrew, meaning 'God is salvation'.

**Josiah**
Hebrew, meaning 'God helps'.

**Josué**
Spanish variant of Joshua, meaning 'God is salvation'.

**Jovan**
Latin, meaning 'the supreme God'.

**Joyce**
Latin, meaning 'joy'.

**Juan**
Spanish variant of John, meaning 'God is gracious'.

**Jubal**
Hebrew, meaning 'ram's horn'.

**Jude**
Hebrew, meaning 'praise' or 'thanks'.

**Judson**
Variant of Jude, meaning 'praise' or 'thanks'.

**Jules**
From Julian, meaning 'Jove's child'.

**Julian**
(alt. Julio)
Greek, meaning 'Jove's child'.

**J**

## 'Bad boy' names

Ace
Arnie
Axel
Bruce
Buzz
Conan
Guy
Rhett
Spike
Tyson

### Julien
French variant of Julian, meaning 'Jove's child'.

### Junior
Latin, meaning 'the younger one'.

### Junius
Latin, meaning 'young'.

### Jupiter
Latin, meaning 'the supreme God'. Jupiter was king of the Roman gods and the god of thunder.

### Juraj
Hebrew, meaning 'God is my judge'.

### Jurgen
Greek, meaning 'farmer'.

### Justice
English, from the word 'justice'.

### Justin
(alt. Justus)

Latin, meaning 'just and upright'.

### Juwan
Hebrew, meaning 'the Lord is gracious'.

**J**

## Famous male guitarists

Brian (May)
Carlos (Santana)
Chuck (Berry)
Eddie (Van Halen)
Eric (Clapton)
Frank (Zappa)
Jeff (Beck)
Jimi/Jimmy (Hendrix/Page)
Joe (Satriani)
Keith (Richards)

# K Boys' names

### Kabelo
African, meaning 'gift'.

### Kade
Scottish, meaning 'from the wetlands'.

### Kadeem
Arabic, meaning 'one who serves'.

### Kaden
*(alt. Kadin, Kaeden, Kaedin, Kaiden)*
Arabic, meaning 'companion'.

### Kadir
Arabic, meaning 'capable and competent'.

### Kahekili
Hawaiian, meaning 'the thunder'.

### Kahlil
Arabic, meaning 'friend'.

### Kai
Greek, meaning 'keeper of the keys'.

### Kaito
Japanese, meaning 'ocean and sake dipper'.

### Kalani
Hawaiian, meaning 'sky'.

### Kale
German, meaning 'free man'.

### Kaleb
Hebrew, meaning 'dog' or 'aggressive'.

### Kalen
*(alt. Kaelen, Kalan)*
Gaelic, meaning 'uncertain'.

**Kaleo**
Hawaiian, meaning 'the voice'.

**Kalil**
Arabic, meaning 'friend'.

**Kalvin**
French, meaning 'bald'.

**Kamari**
Indian, meaning 'the enemy of desire'.

**Kamden**
English, meaning 'winding valley'.

**Kamil**
Arabic, meaning 'perfection'.

**Kane**
Gaelic, meaning 'little battler'.

**Kani**
Hawaiian, meaning 'sound'.

**Kanye**
African town in Botswana. Made popular by rapper Kanye West.

**Kareem**
*(alt. Karim)*
Arabic, meaning 'generous'.

**Karl**
*(alt. Karson)*
Old German, meaning 'free man'.

**Kasey**
*(alt. Kacey)*
Irish, meaning 'alert'.

**Kaspar**
Persian, meaning 'treasurer'.

**Kavon**
Gaelic, meaning 'handsome'.

**Kayden**
Arabic, meaning 'companion'.

**Kazimierz**
Polish, meaning 'declares peace'.

**Kazuki**
Japanese, meaning 'radiant hope'.

**K**

## Kazuo

Japanese, meaning 'harmonious man'.

## Keagan

*(alt. Keegan, Kegan)*
Gaelic, meaning 'small flame'.

## Keane

Gaelic, meaning 'fighter'.

## Keanu

Hawaiian, meaning 'breeze'.

## Keary

Gaelic, meaning 'black-haired'.

## Keaton

English, meaning 'place of hawks'.

## Keeler

Gaelic, meaning 'beautiful and graceful'.

## Keenan

*(alt. Kenan)*
Gaelic, meaning 'little ancient one'.

## Keiji

Japanese, meaning 'govern with discretion'.

## Keir

Gaelic, meaning 'dark-haired' or 'dark-skinned'.

## Keith

Gaelic, meaning 'woodland'.

## Kekoa

Hawaiian, meaning 'brave one' or 'soldier'.

## Kelby

Old English, meaning 'farmhouse near the stream'.

## Kell

*(alt. Kellan, Kellen, Kelley, Kelly, Kiel)*
Norse, meaning 'spring'.

## Kelsey

Old English, meaning 'victorious ship'.

## Kelton

Old English, meaning 'town of the keels'.

137

**K**

### Kelvin
Old English, meaning 'friend of ships'.

### Ken
Shortened form of Kenneth, meaning 'born of fire'.

### Kendal
Old English, meaning 'the Kent river valley'.

### Kendon
Old English, meaning 'brave guard'.

### Kendrick
Gaelic, meaning 'royal ruler'.

### Kenelm
Old English, meaning 'bold'.

### Kenji
Japanese, meaning 'intelligent second son'.

### Kennedy
Gaelic, meaning 'helmet head'.

### Kenneth
(alt. Kenney)
Gaelic, meaning 'born of fire'.

### Kennison
English, meaning 'son of Kenneth'.

### Kent
From the English county.

### Kenton
English, meaning 'town of Ken'.

### Kenya
(alt. Kenyon)
From the country in Africa.

### Kenyatta
From Kenya.

### Kenzo
Japanese, meaning 'wise'.

### Keola
Hawaiian, meaning 'life'.

### Keon
(alt. Keoni)
Hawaiian, meaning 'gracious'.

### Kepler
German, meaning 'hat maker'.

**K**

## Kermit
*(alt. Kerwin)*

Gaelic, meaning 'without envy'. Associated with Kermit the Frog.

## Kerr

English, meaning 'wetland'.

## Keshav

Indian, meaning 'beautiful-haired'.

## Kevin

Gaelic, meaning 'handsome beloved'.

## Khalid
*(alt. Khalif, Khalil)*

Arabic, meaning 'immortal'.

## Kian
*(alt. Keyon, Kyan)*

Irish, meaning 'ancient'.

## Kiefer

German, meaning 'barrel maker'.

## Kieran
*(alt. Kieron, Kyron)*

Gaelic, meaning 'black'.

## Kijana

African, meaning 'youth'.

## Kilby

English, from the town of the same name.

## Kilian

Irish, meaning 'bright-headed'.

## Kimani

African, meaning 'beautiful and sweet'.

## King

English, from the word 'king'.

## Kingsley

English, meaning 'the king's meadow'.

## Kirby

German, meaning 'settlement by a church'.

## Kirk

Old German, meaning 'church'.

## Klaus

German, meaning 'victorious'.

# K

## Kobe
*(alt. Koda, Kody)*

Japanese, meaning 'a Japanese city'.

## Kofi
Ghanaian, meaning 'born on Friday'.

## Kohana
Japanese, meaning 'little flower'.

## Kojo
Ghanaian, meaning 'Monday'.

## Kolby
Norse, meaning 'settlement'.

## Korbin
Gaelic, meaning 'a steep hill'.

## Kramer
German, meaning 'shopkeeper'.

## Kris
*(alt. Krish)*

From Christopher, meaning 'bearing Christ inside'.

## Kurt
German, meaning 'courageous advice'.

## Kurtis
French, meaning 'courtier'.

## Kwame
Ghanaian, meaning 'born on Saturday'.

## Kyden
English, meaning 'narrow little fire'.

## Kylan
*(alt. Kyle, Kyleb, Kyler)*

Gaelic, meaning 'narrow and straight'.

## Kyllion
Irish, meaning 'war'.

## Kyree
From Cree, a Canadian tribe.

## Kyros
Greek, meaning 'legitimate power'.

# L Boys' names

### Laban
Hebrew, meaning 'white'.

### Lachlan
Gaelic, meaning 'from the land of lakes'.

### Lacy
Old French, after the place in France.

### Lalit
Hindi, meaning 'beautiful'.

### Lamar
Old German, meaning 'water'.

### Lambert
Scandinavian, meaning 'land brilliant'.

### Lambros
Greek, meaning 'brilliant and radiant'.

### Lamont
Old Norse, meaning 'law man'.

### Lance
French, meaning 'land'.

### Lancelot
Variant of Lance, meaning 'land'. The name of one of the Knights of the Round Table.

### Landen
(alt. Lando, Landon, Landyn, Langdon)
English, meaning 'long hill'.

**L**

## Lane
*(alt. Layne)*
English, from the word 'lanel'.

## Lannie
*(alt. Lanny)*
German, meaning 'precious'.

## Larkin
Gaelic, meaning 'rough' or 'fierce'.

## Laron
French, meaning 'thief'.

## Larry
Latin, from Lawrence, meaning 'man from Laurentum'.

## Lars
Scandinavian variant of Lawrence, meaning 'man from Laurentum'.

## Lasse
Finnish, meaning 'girl'. (Still, ironically, a boy's name.)

## Laszlo
Hungarian, meaning 'glorious rule'.

## Lathyn
Latin, meaning 'fighter'.

## Latif
Arabic, meaning 'gentle'.

## Laurel
Latin, meaning 'bay'.

## Laurent
French, from Lawrence, meaning 'man from Laurentum'.

## Lawrence
Latin, meaning 'man from Laurentum'.

## Lawson
Old English, meaning 'son of Lawrence'.

## Lazarus
Hebrew, meaning 'God is my help'.

## Leandro
Latin, meaning 'lion man'.

## Lear
German, meaning 'of the meadow'.

**L**

### Lee
*(alt. Leigh)*
Old English, meaning 'meadow' or 'valley'.

### Leib
German, meaning 'love'.

### Leif
Scandinavian, meaning 'heir'.

### Leith
From the name of a place in Scotland.

### Lennox
*(alt. Lenny)*
Gaelic, meaning 'with many Elm trees'.

### Leo
Latin, meaning 'lion'.

### Leon
Latin, meaning 'lion'.

### Leonard
Old German, meaning 'lion strength'.

### Leopold
German, meaning 'brave people'.

### Leroy
French, meaning 'king'.

### Lesley
*(alt. Les)*
Scottish, meaning 'holly garden'.

### Lester
English, meaning 'from Leicester'.

### Lewis
French, meaning 'renowned fighter'.

### Liam
German, meaning 'helmet'.

### Lincoln
English, meaning 'lake colony'.

### Lindsay
Scottish, meaning 'linden tree'.

### Linus
Latin, meaning 'lion'.

### Lionel
English, meaning 'lion'.

**L**

## Llewellyn
Welsh, meaning 'like a lion'.

## Lloyd
Welsh, meaning 'gray-haired and sacred'.

## Logan
Gaelic, meaning 'hollow'.

## Lonnie
English, meaning 'lion strength'.

## Lorcan
Gaelic, meaning 'little fierce one'.

## Louis
*(alt. Lou, Louie, Luigi, Luis)*
German, meaning 'famous warrior'.

## Lucas
*(alt. Lukas, Luca)*
English, meaning 'man from Luciana'.

## Lucian
*(alt. Lucio)*
Latin, meaning 'light'.

## Ludwig
German, meaning 'famous fighter'.

## Luke
*(alt. Luc, Luka)*
Latin, meaning 'from Lucanus' (in southern Italy).

## Lupe
Latin, meaning 'wolf'.

## Luther
German, meaning 'soldier of the people'.

## Lyle
French, meaning 'the island'.

## Lyn
*(alt. Lyndon)*
Spanish, meaning 'pretty'.

# M Boys' names

## Mac
(alt. Mack, Mackie)
Scottish, meaning 'son of'.

## Macaulay
Scottish, meaning 'son of the phantom'.

## Mace
English, meaning 'heavy staff' or 'club'.

## Mackenzie
Scottish, meaning 'the fair one'.

## Mackland
Scottish, meaning 'land of Mac'.

## Macon
French, from the name of towns in France and Georgia.

## Macsen
Scottish, meaning 'son of Mac'.

## Madden
Irish, meaning 'descendant of the hound'.

## Maddox
English, meaning 'good' or 'generous'.

## Madison
(alt. Madsen)
Irish, meaning 'son of Madden'.

## M

**Mads**

Shortened form of Madden, meaning 'descendant of the hound'.

**Magnus**
(alt. Manus)

Latin, meaning 'great'.

**Maguire**

Gaelic, meaning 'son of the beige one'.

**Mahesh**

Hindi, meaning 'great ruler'.

**Mahir**

Arabic, meaning 'skillful'.

**Mahlon**

Hebrew, meaning 'sickness'.

**Mahmoud**

Arabic, meaning 'praise-worthy'.

**Mahoney**

Irish, meaning 'bear'.

**Major**

English, from the word 'major'.

**Makal**

From Michael, meaning 'close to God'.

**Makani**

Hawaiian, meaning 'wind'.

**Makis**

Hebrew, meaning 'gift from God'.

**Mako**

Hebrew, meaning 'God is with us'.

**Malachi**
(alt. Malachy)

Irish, meaning 'messenger of God'.

**Malcolm**

English, meaning 'Columba's servant'.

**Mali**

Arabic, meaning 'full and rich'.

**Manfred**

Old German, meaning 'man of peace'.

## Manish
English, meaning 'manly'.

## Manley
English, meaning 'manly and brave'.

## Mannix
Gaelic, meaning 'little monk'.

## Manoi
*(alt. Manos)*
Japanese, meaning 'love springing from intellect'.

## Manuel
Hebrew, meaning 'God is with us'.

## Manzi
Italian, meaning 'steer'.

## Marc
*(alt. Marco, Marcos, Marcus, Markel)*
French, meaning 'from the god Mars'.

## Marcel
*(alt. Marcelino, Marcello)*
French, meaning 'little warrior'.

## Marek
Polish variant of Mark, meaning 'from the god Mars'.

## Mariano
Latin, meaning 'from the god Mars'.

## Mario
*(alt. Marius)*
Latin, meaning 'manly'.

## Mark
English, meaning 'from the god Mars'.

## Marley
*(alt. Marlin, Marlow)*
Old English, meaning 'meadow near the lake'.

## Marlon
English origin, meaning 'little hawk', made famous by actor Marlon Brando.

## Marshall
Old French, meaning 'caretaker of horses'.

## Martin
*(alt. Marty)*
Latin, meaning 'dedicated to Mars'.

**M**

147

# M

## Marvel

English, from the word 'marvel'.

## Marvin

Welsh, meaning 'sea friend'.

## Mason

English, from the word mason.

## Mathias

*(alt. Matthias)*

Hebrew, meaning 'gift of God'.

## Mathieu

French form of Matthew, meaning 'gift of the Lord'.

## Matthew

Hebrew, meaning 'gift of the Lord'.

## Maurice

*(alt. Mauricio)*

Latin, meaning 'dark skinned' or 'Moorish'.

## Maverick

American, meaning 'non-conformist leader'.

## Max

*(alt. Maxie, Maxim)*

Latin, meaning 'greatest'.

## Maximillian

Latin, meaning 'greatest'.

## Maximino

Latin, meaning 'little Max'.

## Maxwell

Latin, meaning 'Maccus' stream'.

## Maynard

Old German, meaning 'brave'.

## McArthur

Scottish, meaning 'son of Arthur'.

## McCoy

Scottish, meaning 'son of Coy'.

## Mearl

English, meaning 'my earl'.

## Mederic

French, meaning 'doctor'.

**M**

## Mekhi

African, meaning 'who is God?'.

## Mel

Gaelic, meaning 'smooth brow'.

## Melbourne

From the city in Australia.

## Melchior

Persian, meaning 'king of the city'.

## Melton

English, meaning 'town of Mel'.

## Melva

Hawaiian, meaning 'plumeria'.

## Melville

Scottish, meaning 'town of Mel'.

## Melvin

*(alt. Melvyn)*

English, meaning 'smooth brow'.

## Memphis

Greek, meaning 'established and beautiful'.

## Mercer

English, from the word 'mercer'.

## Merl

French, meaning 'blackbird'.

## Merlin

Welsh, meaning 'sea fortress'.

## Merrick

Welsh, meaning 'Moorish'.

## Merrill

Gaelic, meaning 'shining sea'.

## Merritt

English, from the word 'merit'.

## Merton

Old English, meaning 'town by the lake'.

## Meyer

Hebrew, meaning 'bright farmer'.

# M

## Michael

Hebrew, meaning 'resembles God'.

## Michalis

*(alt. Miklos)*

Greek form of Michael, meaning 'resembles God'.

## Michel

French form of Michael, meaning 'resembles God'.

## Michelangelo

Italian, meaning 'Michael's angel'. Name of the famous Italian artist.

## Michele

Italian form of Michael, meaning 'resembles God'.

## Miguel

Spanish form of Michael meaning 'resembles God'.

## Mike

*(alt. Mickey, Mikie)*

Shortened form of Michael meaning 'resembles God'.

## Milan

From the name of the Italian city.

## Miles

*(alt. Milo, Milos, Myles)*

English, from the word 'miles'.

## Milton

English, meaning 'miller's town'.

## Miro

Slavic, meaning 'peace'.

## Misha

Russian, meaning 'who is like God'.

## Mitch

Shortened form of Mitchell, meaning 'who is like God'.

## Mitchell

English, meaning 'who is like God'.

## Modesto

Italian, meaning 'modest'.

**M**

## Football players

Bart (Starr)
Deacon (Jones)
Dick (Butkus)
Emmitt (Smith)
Jerry (Rice)
Jim (Brown)
Joe (Namath/Montana)
John/Johnny (Elway
    Unitas)

### Moe
Hebrew, meaning 'God's helmet'.

### Mohamed
*(alt. Mohammad, Mohamet, Mohammed)*
Arabic, meaning 'praiseworthy'.

### Monroe
Gaelic, meaning 'mouth of the river Rotha'.

### Monserrate
Latin, meaning 'jagged mountain'.

### Montague
French, meaning 'pointed hill'.

### Montana
Latin, meaning 'mountain'.

### Monte
Italian, meaning 'mountain'.

### Montgomery
Variant of Montague, meaning 'pointed hill'.

### Monty
Shortened form of Montague, meaning 'pointed hill'.

### Moody
English, from the word 'moody'.

### Mordecai
Hebrew, meaning 'little man'.

### Morgan
Welsh, meaning 'circling sea'.

### Moritz
Latin, meaning 'dark skinned and Moorish'.

### Morpheus
Greek, meaning 'shape'.

**M**

## Morris

Welsh, meaning 'dark-skinned and Moorish'.

## Morrison

English, meaning 'son of Morris'.

## Moroccan

Arabic, meaning 'from Morocco'.

## Mortimer

French, meaning 'dead sea'.

## Morton

Old English, meaning 'moor town'.

## Moses

(alt. Moshe, Moshon)
Hebrew, meaning 'savior'.

## Moss

English, from the word 'moss'.

## Mungo

Gaelic, meaning 'most dear'.

## Murl

French, meaning 'blackbird'.

## Murphy

Irish, meaning 'sea warrior'.

## Murray

Gaelic, meaning 'lord and master'.

## Mustafa

Arabic, meaning 'chosen'.

## Myron

Greek, meaning 'myrrh'.

# N

## Boys' names

### Najee

Arabic, meaning 'dear companion'.

### Nakia

Arabic, meaning 'pure'.

### Nakul

Indian, meaning 'mongoose'.

### Naphtali

Hebrew, meaning 'wrestling'.

### Napoleon

Italian origin, meaning 'man from Naples'. Name of the French general who became Emperor of France.

### Narciso

Latin, from the myth of Narcissus, famous for drowning after gazing at his own reflection.

### Nash

English, meaning 'at the ash tree'.

### Nasir

Arabic, meaning 'helper'.

### Nate

Hebrew, meaning 'God has given'.

### Nathan

(alt. Nathaniel)

Hebrew, meaning 'God has given'.

# N

## Popular song names

Alexander ("Alexander's Ragtime Band", Irving Berlin)
Daniel ("Daniel", Elton John)
Frankie ("Frankie", Sister Sledge)
Jack ("Jumpin' Jack Flash", The Rolling Stones)
James ("James Dean", The Eagles)
Johnny ("Johnny B. Goode", Chuck Berry)
Kenneth ("What's the Frequency, Kenneth?", REM)
Leroy ("Bad, Bad Leroy Brown", Jim Croce)
Mack ("Mack The Knife", Bobby Darin)
Oliver ("Oliver's Army", Elvis Costello)

### Naveen
Indian, meaning 'new'.

### Neal
Irish, meaning 'champion'.

### Ned
Nickname for Edward, meaning 'wealthy guard'.

### Neftali
Hebrew, meaning 'struggling'.

### Nehemiah
Hebrew, meaning 'comforter'.

### Neil
*(alt. Niall)*
Irish, meaning 'champion'.

### Neilson
Irish, meaning 'son of Neil'.

### Nelson
Variant of Neil, meaning 'champion'

### Nemo
Latin, meaning 'nobody'.

### Neo
Latin, meaning 'new'.

**N**

## Nephi
Greek, meaning 'cloud'.

## Nessim
Arabic, meaning 'breeze'.

## Nestor
Greek, meaning 'traveller'.

## Neville
Old French, meaning 'new village'.

## Newton
English, meaning 'new town'.

## Nicholas
(alt. Niklas)
Greek, meaning 'victorious'.

## Nick
(alt. Nico, Niko, Nikos)
Shortened form of Nicholas, meaning 'victorious'.

## Nigel
Gaelic, meaning 'champion'.

## Nikhil
Hindi, meaning 'whole' or 'entire'.

## Nikita
Greek, meaning 'unconquered'. Also a girls' name.

## Nikolai
Russian variant of Nicholas, meaning 'victorious'.

## Nimrod
Hebrew, meaning 'we will rebel'.

## Nissim
Hebrew, meaning 'wonderful things'.

## Noah
Hebrew, meaning 'peaceful'.

## Noel
French, meaning 'Christmas'.

## Nolan
Gaelic, meaning 'champion'.

## Norbert
Old German, meaning 'Northern brightness'.

## N

### Norman

Old German, meaning 'Northerner'.

### Normand

French, meaning 'from Normandy'.

### Norris

Old French, meaning 'Northerner'.

### Norton

English, meaning 'Northern town'.

### Norval

French, meaning 'Northern town'.

### Norwood

English, meaning 'Northern forest'.

### Nova

Latin, meaning 'new'.

### Nuno

Latin, meaning 'ninth'.

### Nunzio

Italian, meaning 'messenger'.

## Names of gods

Anubis (Death: Egyptian)
Apollo (Sun: Roman)
Brahma (Creation: Indian)
Eros (Love: Greek)
Hypnos (Sleep: Greek)
Mars (War: Roman)
Neptune (Sea: Roman)
Ra (Sun: Egyptian)
Shiva (Destruction: Indian)
Vishnu (Preservation: Indian)

 **Boys' names**

## Oakley

English, meaning 'from the oak meadow'.

## Obadiah

Hebrew, meaning 'God's worker'.

## Obama

African, meaning 'crooked'.

## Obed

Hebrew, meaning 'servant of God'.

---

### Spelling options

A vs E (Aiden or Aidan)

F vs PH (Josef or Joseph)

I vs Y (Henri or Henry)

J vs G (Jorge or George)

N vs HN (Jon or John)

QUE vs CK (Frederique or Frederick)

---

## Oberon
Old German, meaning 'royal bear'.

## Obie
Shortened form of Oberon, meaning 'royal bear'.

## Octave
*(alt. Octavian, Octavio)*
Latin, meaning 'eight'.

## Oda
*(alt. Odell, Odie, Odis)*
Hebrew, meaning 'praise God'.

## Ogden
Old English, meaning 'oak valley'.

## Oisin
From the Irish poet.

## Ola
Norse, meaning 'precious'.

## Olaf
*(alt. Olan)*
Old Norse, meaning 'ancestor'.

## Oleander
Hawaiian, meaning 'joyous'.

## Oleg
*(alt. Olen)*
Russian, meaning 'holy'.

## Olin
Russian, meaning 'rock'.

## Oliver
Latin, meaning 'olive tree'.

## Olivier
French form of Oliver, meaning 'olive tree'.

## Ollie
Shortened form of Oliver, meaning 'olive tree'.

## Omar
*(alt. Omari, Omarion)*
Arabic, meaning 'speaker'.

## Ora
Latin, meaning 'hour'.

**O**

## Oran
(alt. Oren, Orrin)
Gaelic, meaning 'light and pale'.

## Orange
English, from the word 'orange'.

## Orion
From the Greek hunter.

## Orlando
(alt. Orlo)
Old German, meaning 'old land'.

## Orpheus
Greek, meaning 'beautiful voice'.

## Orson
Latin, meaning 'bear'.

## Orville
Old French, meaning 'gold town'.

## Osaka
From the Japanese city.

## Osborne
Norse, meaning 'bear god'.

## Oscar
Old English, meaning 'spear of the gods'.

## Oswald
German, meaning 'God's power'.

---

## Foreign alternatives

David (Dafydd, Dann)
John (Jean, Juan)
Joseph (Giuseppe, José)
Michael (Miguel, Mikhail)
Owen (Eoghan, Owain)
Peter (Pedro, Pierre, Pieter)
Richard (Ricardo)

**O**

## Otha
*(alt. Otho)*
German, meaning 'wealth'.

## Othello
Old German, meaning 'wealth'.
From the Shakespearean
character.

## Otis
German, meaning 'wealth'.

## Otten
English, meaning 'otter-like'.

## Otto
Italian, meaning 'eight'.

## Owain
Welsh, meaning 'youth'.

## Owen
Welsh, meaning 'well born and
noble'.

## Oz
Hebrew, meaning 'strength'.

---

### Popular Asian names for boys and girls

Bao
Cái
Huang
Jiro
Kei
Ming
Miyoko
Shen
Tai
Yoko

# P

**Boys' names**

### Pablo
Spanish, meaning 'little'.

### Padma
Indian, meaning 'lotus'.

### Padraig
Irish, meaning 'noble'.

### Panos
Greek, meaning 'all holy'.

### Paolo
Italian, meaning 'little'.

### Paresh
Indian, meaning 'supreme standard'.

### Parker
Old English, meaning 'park keeper'.

### Pascal
Latin, meaning 'Easter child'.

### Pat
Shortened form of Patrick, meaning 'noble'.

### Patrick
*(alt. Patrice)*
Irish, meaning 'noble'.

### Patten
English, meaning 'noble'.

### Paul
Hebrew, meaning 'small'.

**P**

**Pavel**

Latin, meaning 'small'.

**Pax**

Latin, meaning 'peace'.

**Paxton**

English, meaning 'town of peace'.

**Payne**

Latin, meaning 'peasant'.

**Payton**

Latin, meaning 'peasant's town'.

**Pedro**

Spanish form of Peter, meaning 'rock'.

**Penn**

English, meaning 'hill'.

**Percival**

French, meaning 'pierce the valley'.

**Percy**

Shortened form of Percival, meaning 'pierce the valley'.

**Perez**

Hebrew, meaning 'breach'.

**Pericles**

Greek, meaning 'far-famed'.

**Perrin**

Greek, meaning 'rock'.

**Perry**

English, meaning 'rock'.

**Pervis**

English, meaning 'purveyor'.

**Pete**

Shortened form of Peter, meaning 'rock'.

**Peter**

Greek, meaning 'rock'.

**Petros**

Greek form of Peter, meaning 'rock'.

**Peyton**

Old English, meaning 'fighting man's estate'.

**P**

## Phil

Shortened form of Philip, meaning 'lover of horses'.

## Philip

Greek, meaning 'lover of horses'.

## Philo

Greek, meaning 'love'.

## Phineas

*(alt. Pinchas)*

Hebrew, meaning 'oracle'.

## Phoenix

Greek, meaning 'dark red'.

## Pierre

French form of Peter, meaning 'rock'.

## Piers

Greek form of Peter, meaning 'rock'.

## Pierson

Variant of Pierce, meaning 'son of Piers'.

## Pip

Greek, meaning 'lover of horses'.

## Placido

Latin, meaning 'placid'.

## Pradeep

Hindi, meaning 'light'.

## Pranav

Hindi, meaning 'spiritual leader'.

## Presley

Old English, meaning 'priest's meadow'.

## Preston

Old English, meaning 'priest's town'.

---

## No-nickname names

Alex
Jude
Keith
Otto
Owen
Toby

---

**P**

### Primo
Italian, meaning 'first'.

### Primus
Latin, meaning 'first'.

### Prince
English, from the word 'prince'.

### Prospero
Latin, meaning 'prosperous'.

### Pryce
*(alt. Prize)*
Old French, meaning 'prize'.

### Pryor
English, meaning 'first'.

### Ptolemy
Greek, meaning 'aggressive' or 'warlike'.

# Boys' names

**Quabil**

Arabic, meaning 'able'.

**Quadim**

Arabic, meaning 'able'.

**Quadir**

Arabic, meaning 'powerful'.

**Quaid**

Irish, meaning 'fourth'.

**Quemby**

Norse, meaning 'from the woman's estate'.

**Quentin**

*(alt. Quinten, Quintin, Quinton, Quintus)*

Latin, meaning 'fifth'.

**Quillan**

Gaelic, meaning 'sword'.

**Quillon**

Gaelic, meaning 'club'.

**Quincy**

Old French, meaning 'estate of the fifth son'.

**Quinlan**

Gaelic, meaning 'fit, shapely and strong'.

**Quinn**

Gaelic, meaning 'counsel'.

## 'Powerful' names

| | |
|---|---|
| Americo | Oswald |
| Derek | Oz |
| Hercules | Roderick |
| Michio | Thor |

# R Boys' names

**Radames**

Slavic, meaning 'famous joy'.

**Raekwon**

Hebrew, meaning 'God has healed'.

**Rafael**

*(alt. Rafe, Rafer, Raffi, Raphael)*

Hebrew, meaning 'God has healed'.

**Ragnar**

Old Norse, meaning 'judgement warrior'.

**Raheem**

Arabic, meaning 'merciful and kind'.

**Rahm**

Hebrew, meaning 'pleasing'.

**Rahul**

*(alt. Raoul, Raul)*

Indian, meaning 'efficient'.

**Raiden**

*(alt. Rainen)*

From the Japanese god of thunder.

**Rainen**

Old German, meaning 'deciding warrior'.

**Raj**

Indian, meaning 'king'.

**Rajesh**

*(alt. Ramesh)*

Indian, meaning 'ruler of kings'.

**Raleigh**

Old English, meaning 'deer's meadow'.

# R

**Ralph**

Old English, meaning 'wolf'.

**Ram**

English, from the word 'ram'.

**Ramiro**

Germanic, meaning 'powerful in battle'.

**Ramsey**

(alt. Ramsay)

Old English, meaning 'wild garlic island'.

**Randall**

(alt. Randolph)

Old German, meaning 'wolf shield'.

**Randy**

Variant of Randall, meaning 'wolf shield'. In modern English, randy can also mean amorous.

**Raniel**

English, meaning 'God is my happiness'.

**Ranjit**

Indian, meaning 'influenced by charm'.

**Rannoch**

Gaelic, meaning 'fern'.

**Rashad**

Arabic, meaning 'good judgment'.

**Rasheed**

(alt. Rashid)

Indian, meaning 'rightly guided'.

**Rasmus**

Greek, meaning 'beloved'.

**Raven**

English, from the word 'raven'.

**Ravi**

French, meaning 'delighted'.

**Ray**

English, from the word 'ray'.

**Raymond**

(alt. Rayner)

English, meaning 'advisor'.

**Raz**

Israeli, meaning 'secret' or 'mystery'.

**R**

## Reagan
Irish, meaning 'little king'.

## Reggie
Latin, meaning 'queen'.

## Reginald
Latin, meaning 'regal'.

## Regis
Shortened form of Reginald, meaning 'regal'.

## Reid
Old English, meaning 'by the reeds'.

## Reilly
English, meaning 'courageous'.

## Remus
Latin, meaning 'swift'.

## Rémy
French, meaning 'from Rheims'.

## Ren
Shortened form of Reginald, meaning 'regal'.

## Renato
Latin, meaning 'rebirth'.

## Rene
French, meaning 'rebirth'.

## Reno
Latin, meaning 'renewed'.

## Reuben
Spanish, meaning 'a son'.

## Reuel
Hebrew, meaning 'friend of God'.

## Rex
Latin, meaning 'king'.

## Rey
Spanish, meaning 'king'.

## Reynold
Latin, meaning 'king's advisor'.

## Rhodes
German, meaning 'where the roses grow'. Also the name of the Greek town.

## Rhodri
Welsh, meaning 'ruler of the circle'.

# R

## Rhys
(alt. Reece, Riece)
Welsh, meaning 'enthusiasm'.

## Richard
(alt. Ricardo, Rikardo)
Old German, meaning
'powerful leader'.

## Richie
Shortened form of Richard,
meaning 'powerful leader'.

## Ricky
(alt. Ricki)
Shortened form of Richard,
meaning 'powerful leader'.

## Ridley
English, meaning 'cleared
wood'.

## Rigby
English, from the place in
Lancashire.

## Riky
Irish Gaelic, meaning
'courageous'.

## Ringo
English, meaning 'ring'.

## Rio
Spanish, meaning 'river'.

## Riordan
Gaelic, meaning 'bard'.

## Rishi
Variant of Richard, meaning
'powerful leader'.

## Ritchie
Shortened form of Richard,
meaning 'powerful leader'.

## Roald
Scandinavian, meaning 'ruler'.

## Rob
(alt. Robbie)
Shortened form of Robert,
meaning 'bright fame'.

## Robert
Old German, meaning 'bright
fame'.

## Roberto
Variant of Robert, meaning
'bright fame'.

## Robin
English, from the word 'robin'.

## Robinson

English, meaning 'son of Robin'.

## Rocco

*(alt. Rocky)*

Italian, meaning 'rest'.

## Rod

Short for both Rhodri and Rodney.

## Roderick

German, meaning 'famous power'.

## Rodney

Old German, meaning 'island near the clearing'.

## Rodrigo

Spanish form of Roderick, meaning 'famous power'.

## Roger

Old German, meaning 'spear man'.

## Roland

Old German, meaning 'renowned land'.

## Rolf

Old German, meaning 'wolf'.

**R**

## Rollie

*(alt. Rollo)*

Old German, meaning 'renowned land'.

## Roman

Latin, meaning 'from Rome'.

## Romeo

Latin, meaning 'pilgrim to Rome'. Made famous by Shakespeare's play.

## Ron

*(alt. Ronnie)*

Shortened form of Ronald, meaning 'mountain of strength'.

## Ronald

Norse, meaning 'mountain of strength'.

## Ronan

Gaelic, meaning 'little seal'.

## Rory

English, meaning 'red king'.

# R

### Ross
*(alt. Russ)*
Scottish, meaning 'cape'.

### Rowan
*(alt. Roan)*
Gaelic, meaning 'little red one'.
Also reference to the rowan tree.

### Roy
Gaelic, meaning 'red'.

### Ruben
Hebrew, meaning 'son'.

### Rudolph
Old German, meaning 'famous wolf'.

### Rudy
Shortened form of Rudolph, meaning 'famous wolf'.

### Rufus
Latin, meaning 'red-haired'.

### Rupert
Variant of Robert, meaning 'bright fame'.

### Russell
Old French, meaning 'little red one'.

### Rusty
English, meaning 'ruddy'.

### Ryan
Gaelic, meaning 'little king'.

### Ryder
English, meaning 'horseman'.

### Rye
English, from the word 'rye'.

### Ryker
From Richard, meaning 'powerful leader'.

### Rylan
English, meaning 'land where rye is grown'.

### Ryley
Old English, meaning 'rye clearing'.

# S

# Boys' names

## Saber

French, meaning 'sword'.

## Sagar

African, meaning 'ruler of the water'.

## Sage

English, meaning 'wise'.

## Sakari

Native American, meaning 'sweet'.

## Salim

Arabic, meaning 'secure'.

## Salvador

Spanish, meaning 'savior'.

## Salvatore

Italian, meaning 'savior'.

## Sam

(alt. Sama, Sammie, Sammy)
Hebrew, meaning 'God is heard'. Shortened form of Samuel.

## Samir

Arabic, meaning 'pleasant companion'.

### Spring names

Alvern
Jarek
Kell
Marcus
Tamiko

**S**

## Samson
Hebrew, meaning 'son of Sam'.

## Samuel
Hebrew, meaning 'God is heard'.

## Sandeep
Indian, meaning 'lighting the way'.

## Sandro
Shortened form of Alessandro, meaning 'defending men'.

## Sandy
Shortened form of Alexander, Greek meaning 'defending men'.

## Sanjay
Indian, meaning 'victory'.

## Santana
Spanish, meaning 'saint'.

## Santiago
Spanish, meaning 'Saint James'.

## Santino
Spanish, meaning 'little Saint James'.

## Santo
(alt. Santos)
Latin, meaning 'saint'.

## Sascha
(alt. Sacha, Sasha)
Shortened Russian form of Alexander, meaning 'defending men'.

## Sawyer
English, meaning 'one who saws wood'.

## Scott
(alt. Scottie)
English, meaning 'from Scotland'.

## Seamus
Irish variant of James, meaning 'he who supplants'.

## Sean
(alt. Shaun)
Variant of John, meaning 'God is gracious'.

## Sebastian
Greek, meaning 'revered'.

## Sébastien
French form of Sebastian, meaning 'revered'.

**S**

**Sergio**
Latin, meaning 'servant'.

**Seth**
Hebrew, meaning 'appointed'.

**Severus**
Latin, meaning 'severe'.

**Seymour**
English, from the place name in northern France.

**Shane**
Variant of Sean, meaning 'God is gracious'.

**Sharif**
Arabic, meaning 'honored'.

**Shea**
Gaelic, meaning 'admirable'.

**Shelby**
Norse, meaning 'willow'.

**Sherlock**
English, meaning 'fair-haired'.

**Sherman**
Old English, meaning 'shear man'.

**Shmuel**
Hebrew, meaning 'his name is God'.

**Shola**
Arabic, meaning 'energetic'.

**Sid**
Shortened form of Sidney, meaning 'wide meadow'.

**Sidney**
English, meaning 'wide meadow'.

**Sigmund**
Old German, meaning 'victorious hand'.

**Silvanus**
(alt. Silvio)
Latin, meaning 'woods'.

---

## Summer names

Augustus
Balder
Leo
Sky
Somers

---

**S**

### Sim

Swahili, shortened form of Simba, meaning 'lion'.

### Simba

Swahili, meaning 'lion'.

### Simon

*(alt. Simeon)*

Hebrew, meaning 'to hear'.

### Sinbad

Literary merchant adventurer.

### Sindri

Norse, meaning 'dwarf'.

### Sipho

African, meaning 'the unknown one'.

### Sire

English, from the word 'sire'.

### Sirius

Hebrew, meaning 'brightest star'.

### Skipper

English, meaning 'ship captain'.

### Skyler

Dutch, meaning 'guarded' or 'scholar'.

### Solomon

Hebrew, meaning 'peace'.

### Sonny

American English, meaning 'son'.

### Soren

Scandinavian, meaning 'brightest star'.

### Spencer

English, meaning 'dispenser'.

### Spike

English, from the word 'spike'.

### Stan

Shortened form of Stanley, meaning 'stony meadow'.

### Stanford

English, meaning 'stone ford'.

### Stanley

English, meaning 'stony meadow'.

**S**

**Stavros**

Greek, meaning 'crowned'.

**Stellan**

Latin, meaning 'starred'.

**Steno**

German, meaning 'stone'.

**Stephen**

(alt. Stefan, Stefano, Steffan)
English, meaning 'crowned'.

**Steven**

(alt. Steve, Stevie)
English, meaning 'crowned'.

**Stewart**

English, meaning 'steward'.

**Stoney**

English, meaning 'stone like'.

**Storm**

English, from the word 'storm'.

**Stuart**

English, meaning 'steward'.

**Sven**

Norse, meaning 'boy'.

**Sydney**

English, meaning 'wide meadow'. Also a city in Australia.

**Syed**

Arabic, meaning 'lucky'.

**Sylvester**

Latin, meaning 'wooded'.

## Autumn names

Aki
Akiko
Demitrius
George
Goren

**S**

## Popular Australian names for boys and girls

| | |
|---|---|
| Adelaide | Hobart |
| Brad | Lorrae |
| Darwin | Narelle |
| Evonne | Raelene |
| Griffith | Tallara |

# T

## Boys' names

### Tacitus

Latin, meaning 'silent, calm', from the Roman historian.

### Tad

English, from the word 'tadpole'.

### Taj

Indian, meaning 'crown'.

### Takashi

Japanese, meaning 'praiseworthy'.

### Takoda

Sioux, meaning 'friend to everyone'.

### Talbot

(alt. Tal)

Aristocratic English name.

### Tamir

Arabic, meaning 'tall and wealthy'.

### Tanner

Old English, meaning 'leather-maker'.

### Taras

(alt. Tarez)

Scottish, meaning 'crag'.

### Tarek

Arabic, meaning 'evening caller'.

### Tarian

Welsh, meaning 'silver'.

### Tariq

Arabic, meaning 'morning star'.

# T

## Tarquin

Latin, from the Roman clan name.

## Tarun

Hindi, meaning 'young'.

## Tatanka

Hebrew, meaning 'bull'.

## Tate

English, meaning 'cheerful'.

## Taurean

English, meaning 'bull-like'.

## Tavares

English, meaning 'descendant of the hermit'.

## Tave

(alt. Tavian, Tavis, Tavish)

French, from Gustave, meaning 'royal staff'.

## Taylor

English, meaning 'tailor'.

## Ted

(alt. Teddy)

English, from Edward, meaning 'wealthy guard'.

## Terence

(alt. Terrill, Terry)

English, meaning 'tender'.

## Tex

English, meaning 'Texan'.

## Thane

(alt. Thayer)

Scottish, meaning 'landholder'.

## Thatcher

(alt. Thaxter)

Old English, meaning 'roof thatcher'.

## Thelonius

Latin, meaning 'ruler of the people'.

## Theo

Shortened form of Theodore, meaning 'God's gift'.

## Theodore

Greek, meaning 'God's gift'.

## Theophile

Latin, meaning 'God's love'.

## Theron

Greek, meaning 'hunter'.

**T**

**Thierry**
French variant of Terence, meaning 'tender'.

**Thomas**
Aramaic, meaning 'twin'.

**Thomsen**
*(alt. Thomson)*
English, meaning 'son of Thomas'.

**Thor**
Norse, meaning 'thunder'.

**Tiago**
From Santiago, meaning 'Saint James'.

**Tiberius**
English, meaning 'from the river Tiber'.

**Tibor**
Latin, from the river Tiber.

**Tiernan**
Gaelic, meaning 'lord'.

**Tilden**
*(alt. Till)*
English, meaning 'fertile valley'.

**Tim**
*(alt. Timmie, Timon)*
Shortened form of Timothy, meaning 'God's honor'.

**Timothy**
Greek, meaning 'God's honor'.

**Tito**
*(alt. Titus, Tizian)*
Latin, meaning 'defender'.

**Tobias**
*(alt. Toby)*
Hebrew, meaning 'God is good'.

**Tod**
*(alt. Todd)*
English, meaning 'fox'.

**Tom**
*(alt. Tomlin, Tommy)*
Aramaic, meaning 'twin'.

**Tonneau**
French, meaning 'barrel'.

**Tony**
Shortened form of Anthony, from the old Roman family name.

# T

## Torey
Norse, meaning 'Thor'.

## Torin
Gaelic, meaning 'chief'.

## Torquil
Gaelic, meaning 'helmet'.

## Toshi
Japanese, meaning 'reflection'.

## Travis
French, meaning 'crossover'.

## Trevor
*(alt. Tvevin)*
Welsh origin, meaning 'great settlement'.

## Trey
*(alt. Tyree)*
French, meaning 'very'.

## Tristan
*(alt. Tristram)*
Celtic from the Celtic hero.

## Troy
Gaelic, meaning 'descended from the soldier'.

## Tudor
Variant of Theodore, 'God's gift'.

## Tyler
English, meaning 'tile maker'.

## Tyrell
French, meaning 'puller'.

## Tyrone
Gaelic, meaning 'Owen's county'.

## Tyson
English, meaning 'son of Tyrone'.

---

## Winter names

Aquilo
Caldwell
Jack
Mistral
Rain

# U

## Boys' names

### Uberto

*(alt. Umberto)*

Italian, variant of Hubert, meaning 'bright or shining intellect'.

### Udo

German, meaning 'power of the wolf'.

### Ugo

Italian form of Hugo, meaning 'mind and heart'.

### Ulf

German, meaning 'wolf'.

### Ulrich

German, meaning 'noble ruler'.

### Ultan

Irish, meaning 'from Ulster'.

### Ulysses

Greek, meaning 'wrathful'. Made famous by the mythological voyager.

### Upton

English, meaning 'high town'.

### Urho

Finnish, meaning 'brave'.

### Uri

*(alt. Uriah, Urias)*

Hebrew, meaning 'my light'.

### Uriel

Hebrew, meaning 'angel of light'.

## Usher

English, from the word 'usher'.
Made famous by the R&B star.

## Uzi

Hebrew, meaning 'my strength'.

## Uzzi

*(alt. Uzziah)*

Hebrew, meaning 'my power'.

## Christmas names

Casper
Celyn
Christian
Gabriel
Jesus
Joseph
Nicholas
Noel

# V

# Boys' names

## Vadim

Russian, meaning 'scandal maker'.

## Valdemar

German, meaning 'renowned leader'.

## Valente

Latin, meaning 'valiant'.

## Valentine

*(alt. Val, Valentin)*

English, from the word 'valentine'.

## Valentino

Italian, meaning 'valentine'.

## Valerio

Italian, meaning 'valiant'.

## Van

Dutch, meaning 'son of'.

## Vance

English, meaning 'marshland'.

## Vangelis

Greek, meaning 'good news'.

## Varro

Latin, meaning 'strong'.

## Varun

Hindi, meaning 'water god'.

## Vasilis

Greek, meaning 'kingly'.

## Vaughan

Welsh, meaning 'little'.

## Vernell

French, meaning 'green and flourishing'.

**V**

**Verner**
German, meaning 'army defender'.

**Vernon**
(alt. Vernie)
French, meaning 'alder grove'.

**Versilius**
Latin, meaning 'flier'.

**Vester**
Latin, meaning 'wooded'.

**Victor**
Latin, meaning 'champion'.

**Vidal**
(alt. Vidar)
Spanish, meaning 'life-giving'.

**Vijay**
Hindi, meaning 'conquering'.

**Vikram**
Hindi, meaning 'sun'.

**Viktor**
Latin, meaning 'victory'.

**Ville**
French, meaning 'town'.

**Vincent**
(alt. Vince)
English, meaning 'victorious'.

**Virgil**
Latin, meaning 'staff bearer'.
From the Latin poet.

**Vito**
Spanish, meaning 'life'.

**Vittorio**
Italian, meaning 'victory'.

**Vitus**
Latin, meaning 'life'.

**Vivian**
Latin, meaning 'lively'.

**Vladimir**
Slavic, meaning 'prince'.

**Volker**
German, meaning 'defender of the people'.

**Von**
Norse, meaning 'hope'.

# Boys' names

## Wade

English, meaning 'to move forward' or 'to go'.

## Waldemar

German, meaning 'famous ruler'.

## Walden

English, meaning 'valley of the Britons'.

## Waldo

Old German, meaning 'rule'.

## Walker

English, meaning 'a fuller'.

## Wallace

English, meaning 'foreigner' or 'stranger'.

## Wally

German, meaning 'ruler of the army'.

## Walter

*(alt. Walt)*

German, meaning 'ruler of the army'.

## Ward

English, meaning 'guardian'.

## Wardell

Old English, meaning 'watchman's hill'.

## Warner

German, meaning 'army guard'.

**W**

### Warren
German, meaning 'guard' or 'the game park'.

### Washington
English, meaning 'clever' or 'clever man's settlement'.

### Wassily
Greek, meaning 'royal' or 'kingly'.

### Watson
English, meaning 'son' or 'son of Walter'.

### Waverley
*(alt. Waverly)*
English, meaning 'quaking aspen'.

### Waylon
English, meaning 'land by the road'.

### Wayne
English, meaning 'a cartwright'.

### Webster
English, meaning 'weaver'.

### Weldon
English, meaning 'from the hill of well' or 'hill with a well'.

### Wendell
*(alt. Wendel)*
German, meaning 'a wend'.

### Werner
German, meaning 'army guard'.

### Weston
English, meaning 'from the west town'.

### Wheeler
English, meaning 'wheel maker'.

### Whitley
English, meaning 'white wood'.

### Whitman
Old English, meaning 'white man'.

### Whitney
Old English, meaning 'white island'.

### Wilber
*(alt. Wilbur)*
Old German, meaning 'bright will'.

### Wiley
Old English, meaning 'beguiling' or 'enchanting'.

### Wilford
Old English, meaning 'the ford by the willows'.

### Wilfredo
*(alt. Wilfred, Wilfrid)*
English, meaning 'to will peace'.

### Wilhelm
German, meaning 'strong-willed warrior'.

### Wilkes
*(alt. Wilkie)*
Old English, meaning 'strong-willed protector' or 'strong and resolute protector'.

### William
*(alt. Will, Willie)*
English (Teutonic), meaning 'strong protector' or 'strong-willed warrior'.

### Willis
English, meaning 'server of William'.

### Willoughby
Old Norse and Old English, meaning 'from the farm by the trees'.

### Wilmer
English (Teutonic), meaning 'famously resolute'.

### Wilmot
English, meaning 'resolute mind'.

### Wilson
English, meaning 'son of William'.

### Wilton
Old Norse and English, meaning 'from the farm by the brook/streams'.

### Windell
*(alt. Wendell)*
German, meaning 'wanderer' or 'seeker'.

## Windsor

Old English, meaning 'river bank' or 'landing place'.

## Winfield

English, meaning 'from the field of Wina'.

## Winslow

Old English, meaning 'victory on the hill'.

## Winter

Old English, meaning 'to be born in the winter'.

## Winthrop

Old English, meaning 'village of friends'.

## Winton

Old English, meaning 'a friend's farm'.

## Wirrin

Aboriginal, meaning 'a tea tree'.

## Wistan

Old English, meaning 'battle stone' or 'mark of the battle'.

---

### Food-inspired names

Ale
Basil
Berry
Cane
Chuck
Graham
Herb
Kale
Reuben
Rye
Shad
Tamir

---

## Wittan

Old English, meaning 'farm in the woods' or 'farm by the woods'.

## Wolf

*(alt. Wolfe)*

English, meaning 'strong as a wolf'.

## Wolfgang

Teutonic, meaning 'the path of wolves'.

## Wolfrom

Teutonic, meaning 'raven wolf'.

## Wolter

Dutch, a form of Walter meaning 'ruler of the army'.

## Woodburn

Old English, meaning 'a stream in the woods'.

## Woodrow

English, meaning 'from the row of houses by the wood'.

## Woodward

English, meaning 'guardian of the forest'.

## Woody

American, meaning 'path in the woods'.

## Worcester

Old English, meaning 'from a Roman site'.

## Worth

American, meaning 'worth much' or 'wealthy place' or 'wealth and riches'.

## Wren

Old English, meaning 'tiny bird'.

## Wright

Old English, meaning 'to be a craftsman' or 'from a carpenter'.

## Wyatt

Teutonic, meaning 'from wood' or 'from the wide water'.

## Wynn

*(alt. Wyn)*

Welsh, meaning 'very blessed' or 'the fair blessed one'.

## Popular English names for boys and girls

| | |
|---|---|
| Ada | Julian |
| Darren | Lana |
| Dudley | Lauren |
| Faith | Posy |
| Garrett | Rodney |

# X Boys' names

## Xadrian

American, a combination of X and Adrian, meaning 'from Hadria'.

## Xander

Greek, meaning 'defender of the people'.

## Xanthus

Greek, meaning 'golden-haired'.

## Xavier

Latin, meaning 'to the new house'.

## Xenon

Greek, meaning 'the guest'.

## Xerxes

Persian, meaning 'ruler of the people' or 'respected king'.

## Xylander

Greek, meaning 'man of the forest'.

## Bird names

Drake
Efron
Gannet
Jay
Robin

## Popular names of Presidents

Abraham (Lincoln)
Andrew (Jackson, Johnson)
Barack (Obama)
Franklin (Pierce, Roosevelt)
George (Washington, H. Bush, W. Bush)
James (Madison, Monroe, Knox Polk, Buchanan, Garfield, Carter)
John (Adams, Quincy Adams, Tyler, Kennedy)
Richard (Nixon)
Ronald (Reagan)
William (Henry Harrison, McKinley, Howard Taft, Clinton)

# Y Boys' names

## Yaal

Hebrew, meaning 'ascending' or 'one to ascend'.

## Yadid

Hebrew, meaning 'the beloved one'.

## Yadon

Hebrew, meaning 'against judgment'.

## Yahir

Spanish, meaning 'handsome one'.

## Yair

Hebrew, meaning 'the enlightening one' or 'illuminating'.

## Yakiya

Hebrew, meaning 'pure' or 'bright'.

## Yanis

*(alt. Yannis)*

Greek, a form of John meaning 'gift of God'.

## Yarden

Hebrew, meaning 'to flow downward'.

## Ye

Chinese, meaning 'bright one' or 'light'.

## Yehuda

Hebrew, meaning 'to praise and exalt'.

**Y**

## Yered

Hebrew, a form of Jared, meaning 'descending'.

## Yerik

Russian, meaning 'God-appointed one'.

## Yervant

Armenian, meaning 'king of people'.

## Yitzak
*(alt. Yitzaak)*

Hebrew, meaning 'laughter' or 'one who laughs'.

## Ynyr

Welsh, meaning 'to honor'.

## Yobachi

African, meaning 'one who prays to God' or 'prayed to God'.

## Yogi

Japanese, meaning 'one who practises yoga' or 'from yoga'.

## Yona

Native American, meaning 'bear'; Hebrew, meaning 'dove'.

## York

Celtic, meaning 'yew tree' or 'from the farm of the yew tree'.

## Yosef

Hebrew, meaning 'added by God' or 'God shall add'.

## Yuri

Aboriginal, meaning 'to hear'; Japanese, meaning 'one to listen'; Russian, a form of George meaning 'farmer'.

## Yves

French, meaning 'miniature archer' or 'small archer'.

# Z Boys' names

## Zachariah

*(alt. Zac, Zach, Zachary)*

Hebrew, meaning 'remembered by the Lord' or 'God has remembered'.

## Zad

Persian, meaning 'my son'.

## Zadok

Hebrew, meaning 'righteous one'.

## Zador

Hungarian, meaning 'violent demeanor'.

## Zafar

Arabic, meaning 'triumphant'.

## Zaid

African, meaning 'increase the growth' or 'growth'.

## Zaide

Yiddish, meaning 'the elder ones'.

## Zain

*(alt. Zane)*

Arabic, meaning 'the handsome son'.

## Zaire

African, meaning 'river from Zaire'.

## Zander

Greek, meaning 'defender of my people'.

**Z**

### Zarek

Persian, meaning 'God protect our King'.

## Names from nature

Ash
Condor
Flint
River
Tiger

# part three

# Girls’
# Names

# A Girls' names

## A'mari

Variation of the Swahili or Muslim name Amira, meaning 'princess'.

## Aanya

Variation of the Russian name Anya, meaning 'favor' or 'grace'. Also of Sanskrit origin, meaning 'the inexhaustible'.

## Aaryanna

Derivative of the Latin and Greek name Ariadne meaning 'the very holy one'.

## Abby
*(alt. Abbey, Abbie)*

Form of Abigail, meaning 'my father's joy' in Hebrew.

## Abigail
*(alt. Abagail, Abbigail, Abigale, Abigayle)*

Hebrew, meaning 'my father's joy'.

## Abilene
*(alt. Abilee)*

Variation of Abelena. Latin and Spanish for 'hazelnut'.

## Abra

Female variation of Abraham. Also Sanskrit, meaning 'clouds'.

## Abril

Spanish for the month of April. Also Latin, meaning 'open'.

## Acacia

Greek, meaning 'point' or
'thorn'. Also a species of
flowering trees and shrubs.

## Acadia

Variation of the Greek word
arcadia meaning 'paradise'.
Originally, a French colony in
Canada.

## Ada
*(alt. Adair)*

Hebrew, meaning 'adornment'.

## Adalee

German, meaning 'noble'.

## Adalia

Hebrew, meaning 'God is my
refuge'.

## Addie
*(alt. Addy, Adi)*

Shortened form of Addison,
Adelaide, Adele and Adeline.

## Addison
*(alt. Addisyn, Addyson)*

English, meaning 'son of Adam'.

## Adelaide
*(alt. Adelaida)*

German, popular after the
rule of William IV and Queen
Adelaide of England in the 19th
century.

## Movie inspirations

Anita (*West Side Story*)
Bonnie (*Bonnie & Clyde*)
Dorothy (*The Wizard of Oz*)
Holly (*Breakfast at Tiffany's*)
Judy (*Private Benjamin*)
Leia (*Star Wars*)
Mary (*Mary Poppins*)
Oda Mae (*Ghost*)
Ripley (*Alien*)
Sandy (*Grease*)

### Adele

*(alt. Adela, Adelia, Adell, Adella, Adelle)*

German, meaning 'noble' or 'nobility'.

### Adeline

*(alt. Adalyn, Adalynn, Adelina, Adelyn)*

Variant of Adelaide, meaning 'noble'.

### Aden

*(alt. Addien)*

Hebrew, meaning 'decoration'.

### Aderyn

Welsh, meaning 'bird'.

### Adesina

Nigerian, meaning 'she paves the way'. Usually given to a first-born daughter.

### Adia

Variant of Ada, meaning 'decoration'.

### Adina

*(alt. Adena)*

Hebrew, meaning 'high hopes' or 'precious'.

### Adira

Hebrew, meaning 'noble' or 'powerful'. Also the north Italian city.

### Adrian

Italian, from the northern city of Adria.

### Adrianna

*(alt. Adriana)*

Variant of Adrienne, meaning 'rich' or 'dark'.

### Adrienne

*(alt. Adriane, Adrianne)*

Greek, meaning 'rich', or Latin meaning 'dark'.

### Aegle

Greek, meaning 'brightness' or 'splendor'.

### Aerin

Variant of Erin, meaning 'peace-making'.

### Aerith

American, with no definitive meaning.

## Aero
(alt. Aeron)
Greak, meaning 'water'.

## Aerolynn
Combination of the Greek Aero, meaning 'water', and the English Lynn, meaning 'waterfall'.

## Africa
Celtic, meaning 'pleasant', as well as the name of the continent.

## Afsaneh
Iranian, meaning 'a fairy tale'.

## Afsha
Persian, meaning 'one who sprinkles light'.

## Afton
Originally a place name in Scotland.

## Agatha
From Saint Agatha, the patron saint of bells, meaning 'good'.

## Aglaia
One of the three Greek Graces, meaning 'brilliance'.

## Agnes
Greek, meaning 'virginal' or 'pure'.

## Agrippina
Latin, from the expression, meaning 'born feet first'.

## Aida
Arabic, meaning 'reward' or 'present'.

## Aidanne
(alt. Aidan, Aidenn)
Gaelic, meaning 'fire'.

## Ailbhe
Irish, meaning 'noble' or 'bright'.

## Aileen
(alt. Aelinn, Aleen, Aline, Alline, Eileen)
Gaelic variant of Helen, meaning 'light'.

## Ailith
(alt. Ailish)
Old English, meaning 'seasoned warrior'.

## Ailsa
Scottish, meaning 'pledge from God', as well as the name of a Scottish island.

A

## Aimee

*(alt. Aimie, Amie)*

French form of Amy, meaning 'beloved'.

## Aina

Scandinavian, meaning 'forever'.

## Aine

*(alt. Aino)*

Celtic, meaning 'happiness'.

## Ainsley

Scottish/Gaelic, meaning 'one's own meadow'.

## Aisha

*(alt. Aeysha)*

Arabic, meaning 'woman'; Swahili, meaning 'life'.

## Aishwarya

Variant on Aisha, Arabic, meaning 'woman'.

## Aislinn

*(alt. Aislin, Aisling, Aislyn, Alene, Allene)*

Irish Gaelic, meaning 'dream'.

## Aiyanna

*(alt. Aiyana)*

Native American, meaning 'forever flowering'.

## Aja

Hindi, meaning 'goat'.

## Akela

*(alt. Akilah)*

Hawaiian, meaning 'noble'.

## Akilina

Greek or Russian, meaning 'eagle'.

## Akiva

Hebrew, meaning 'protect and shelter'.

## Alaina

*(alt. Alane, Alani, Alayna, Aleena)*

Feminine of Alan, originating from the Greek for 'rock' or 'comely'.

## Alana

*(alt. Alanna, Alannah)*

Variant of Alaina, meaning 'rock' or 'comely'.

## Alanis

*(alt. Alarice)*

Variant of Alaina, meaning 'rock' or 'comely'.

**A**

## Alba

Latin for 'white'.

## Alberta

*(alt. Albertha, Albertine)*

Feminine of Albert, from the Old German for 'noble, bright, famous'.

## Albina

Latin, meaning 'white' or 'fair'.

## Alda

German, meaning 'old' or 'prosperous'.

## Aldis

English, meaning 'battle-seasoned'.

## Aleta

*(alt. Aletha)*

Greek, meaning 'footloose'.

## Alethea

*(alt. Aletheia)*

Greek, meaning 'truth'.

## Alex

*(alt. Alexa, Alexi, Alexia, Alexina)*

Shortened version of Alexandra, meaning 'man's defender'.

## Alexandra

*(alt. Alejandra, Alejandrina, Alejhandra, Aleksandra, Alessandra, Alexandrea, Alexandria, Aliandra)*

Feminine of Alexander, from the Greek interpretation of 'man's defender'.

## Alexis

*(alt. Alexus, Alexys)*

Greek, meaning 'helper'.

## Aleydis

Variant of Alice, meaning 'nobility'.

## Alfreda

Old English, meaning 'elf power'.

## Ali

*(alt. Allie, Ally)*

Shortened version of Alexandra, Aliyah or Alice.

## Alibeth

Variant of Elizabeth, meaning 'pledged to God'.

## Alice

*(alt. Alize, Alyce, Alys, Alyse)*

English, meaning 'noble' or 'nobility'.

A

## Alicia

*(alt. Ahlicia, Alecia, Alesia,
Alessia, Alizia, Alycia, Alysia)*

Variant of Alice, meaning
'nobility'.

## Alida

*(alt. Aleida)*

Latin, meaning 'small-winged
one'.

## Alienor

*(alt. Aliana)*

Variant spelling of Eleanor.
Greek, meaning 'light'.

## Aliki

*(alt. Alika)*

Variant of Alice, meaning
'nobility'.

## Alima

Arabic, meaning 'cultured'.

## Alina

*(alt. Alena)*

Slavic, variation of Helen,
meaning 'light'.

## Alisha

*(alt. Alesha, Alysha)*

Variant of Alice, meaning
'nobility'.

## Alison

*(alt. Allison, Allisyn, Allyson,
Alyson)*

Variant of Alice, meaning
'nobility'.

## Alivia

Variant of Olivia, meaning
'olive tree'.

## Aliya

*(alt. Aaliyah, Aleah, Alia, Aliah,
Aliyah)*

Arabic, meaning 'exalted' or
'sublime'.

## Alla

Variant of Ella or Alexandra.
Also a possible reference to
Allah.

## Allegra

Italian, meaning 'joyous'.

## Allura

French, from the word for
entice, meaning 'the power of
attraction'.

## Allyn

Feminine of Alan, meaning
'peaceful'.

A

### Alma

Three possible origins: Latin for 'giving nurture', Italian for 'soul' and Arabic for 'learned'.

### Almeda
(alt. Almeta)

Latin, meaning 'ambitious'.

### Almera
(alt. Almira)

Feminine of Elmer, from the Arabic for 'aristocratic' and the Old English meaning 'noble'.

### Alohi

Variant of the Hawaiian greeting Aloha, meaning 'love and affection'.

### Alona

Hebrew, meaning 'oak tree'.

### Alora

Variant of Alona, meaning 'oak tree'.

### Alpha

The first letter of the Greek alphabet, usually given to a firstborn daughter.

### Alta

Latin, meaning 'elevated'.

### Altagracia

Spanish, meaning 'grace'.

### Althea
(alt. Altea, Altha)

Greek, meaning 'healing power'.

### Alva

Spanish, meaning 'blonde' or 'fair-skinned'.

### Alvena
(alt. Alvina)

English, meaning 'noble friend'.

### Alvia
(alt. Alyvia)

Variant of Olivia or Elvira.

### Alyssa
(alt. Alisa, Alissa, Allyssa, Alysa)

Greek, meaning 'rational'.

### Amabel

Variant of Annabel, meaning 'grace and beauty'.

### Amadea

Feminine of Amadeus, meaning 'God's' love.

**A**

### Amalia

Variant of Emilia, Latin, meaning 'rival, eager'.

### Amana

Hebrew, meaning 'loyal and true'.

### Amanda

Latin, meaning 'much loved'.

### Amandine

Variant of Amanda, meaning 'much loved'.

### Amara

*(alt. Amani)*

Greek, meaning 'lovely forever'.

### Amarantha

Contraction of Amanda and Samantha, meaning 'much loved listener'.

### Amaris

*(alt. Amari, Amasa, Amata, Amaya)*

Hebrew, meaning 'pledged by God'.

### Amaryllis

Greek, meaning 'fresh'. Also a flower by the same name.

### Amber

French, from the semi-precious stone of the same name.

### Amberly

Contraction of Amber and Leigh, meaning 'stone' and 'meadow'.

### Amberlynn

Contraction of Amber and Lynn, meaning 'stone' and 'waterfall'.

### Amelia

*(alt. Aemilia)*

Greek, meaning 'industrious'.

### Amelie

*(alt. Amalie)*

French version of Amelia, meaning 'industrious'.

### America

From the country of the same name.

### Ameris

Variant of amaryllis, meaning 'fresh'.

## Amethyst

Greek, from the precious, mulberry colored stone of the same name.

## Amina

Arabic, meaning 'honest and trustworthy'.

## Amira

(alt. Amiya, Amiyah)

Arabic, meaning 'a high-born girl'.

## Amity

Latin, meaning 'friendship and harmony'.

## Amory

Variant of the Spanish name Amor, meaning 'love'.

## Amy

(alt. Amee, Ami, Amie, Ammie)

Latin, meaning 'beloved'.

## Amya

Variant of Amy, meaning 'beloved'.

## Ana-Lisa

Contraction of Anna and Lisa, meaning 'grace' or 'consecrated to God'.

## Anafa

Hebrew, meaning 'heron'.

## Ananda

Hindi, meaning 'bliss'.

## Anastasia

(alt. Athanasia)

Greek, meaning 'resurrection'.

## Anatolia

From the eastern Greek town of the same name.

## Andrea

(alt. Andreia, Andria)

Feminine of Andrew, from the Greek term for 'a man's woman'.

## Andrine

Variant of Andrea, meaning 'a man's woman'.

## Andromeda

From the heroine of a Greek legend.

## Anemone

Greek, meaning 'breath'.

## Angela
*(alt. Angel, Angeles, Angelia*
*Angelle, Angie)*
Greek, meaning 'messenger
from God' or 'angel'.

## Angelica
*(alt. Angelina, Angeline,*
*Angelique, Angelise, Angelita,*
*Anjelica)*
Latin, meaning 'angelic'.

## Anise
*(alt. Anisa, Anissa)*
French, from the licorice
flavored plant of the same name.

## Aniston
English, meaning 'town of Agnes'.

## Anita
*(alt. Anitra)*
Variant of Ann, meaning 'grace'.

## Ann
*(alt. Anne, Annie)*
Derived from Hannah,
meaning 'grace'.

## Anna
*(alt. Ana, Anne)*
Derived from Hannah,
meaning 'grace'.

## Annabel
*(alt. Anabel, Anabelle, Annabell,*
*Annabella, Annabelle)*
Contraction of Anna and
Belle, meaning 'grace' and
'beauty'.

## Annalise
*(alt. Annalee, Annalisa, Anneli,*
*Annelie, Annelise)*
Contraction of Anna and Lise,
meaning 'grace' and 'pledged
to God'.

## Annemarie
*(alt. Annamae, Annamarie,*
*Annelle, Annmarie)*
Contraction of Anna and Mary,
meaning 'grace' and 'star of the
sea'.

## Annette
*(alt. Annetta)*
Derived from Hannah, Hebrew,
meaning 'grace'.

## Annis
Greek, meaning 'finished or
completed'.

## Annora
Latin, meaning 'honor'.

**A**

### Anoushka
*(alt. Anousha)*

Russian variation of Ann, meaning 'grace'.

### Ansley

English, meaning 'the awesome one's meadow'.

### Anthea
*(alt. Anthi)*

Greek, meaning 'flower-like'.

### Antigone

In Greek mythology, Antigone was the daughter of Oedipus.

### Antoinette
*(alt. Anonetta, Antonette, Antonietta)*

Both a variation of Ann and the feminine of Anthony, meaning 'invaluable grace'.

### Antonia
*(alt. Antonella, Antonina)*

Latin, meaning 'invaluable'.

### Anwen

Welsh, meaning 'very fair'.

### Anya
*(alt. Aniya, Aniyah, Aniylah, Anja)*

Russian, meaning 'grace'.

### Aoife

Gaelic, meaning 'beautiful joy'.

### Apollonia

Feminine of Apollo, the Greek god of the sun.

### Apple

From the name of the fruit.

### April
*(alt. Avril)*

Latin, meaning 'opening up'. Also the name of the month.

### Aquilina
*(alt. Aqua, Aquila)*

Spanish, meaning 'like an eagle'.

### Ara

Arabic, meaning 'brings rain'.

### Arabella

Latin, meaning 'answered prayer'.

### Araceli
*(alt. Aracely)*

Spanish, meaning 'altar of Heaven'.

## Araminta

Contraction of Arabella and Amita, meaning 'altar of Heaven' and 'friendship'.

## Arcadia

Greek, meaning 'paradise'.

## Ardelle

(alt. Ardell, Ardella)

Latin, meaning 'burning with enthusiasm'.

## Arden

(alt. Ardis, Ardith)

Latin, meaning 'burning with enthusiasm'.

## Arella

(alt. Areli, Arely)

Hebrew, meaning 'angel'.

## Aretha

Greek, meaning 'woman of virtue'.

## Aria

(alt. Ariah)

Italian, meaning 'melody'.

## Ariadne

Both Greek and Latin, meaning 'the very holy one'. In Greek mythology, Ariadne was the daughter of King Minos.

## Ariana

(alt. Ariane, Arianna, Arienne)

Welsh, meaning 'silver'.

## Ariel

(alt. Ariela, Ariella, Arielle)

Hebrew, meaning 'lioness of God'.

## Arlene

(alt. Arleen, Arlie, Arline, Arly)

Gaelic, meaning 'pledge'.

## Armida

Latin, meaning 'little armed one'.

## Artemisia

(alt. Artemis)

Greek/Spanish, meaning 'perfect'.

## Artie

(alt. Arti)

Shortened form of Artemisia, meaning 'perfect'.

**A**

### Ashanti

Geographical area in Africa

### Ashby

English, meaning 'ash tree farm'.

### Ashley

*(alt. Ashlee, Ashleigh, Ashli, Ashlie, Ashly)*

English, meaning 'ash tree meadow'.

### Ashlynn

*(alt. Ashlyn)*

Irish Gaelic, meaning 'dream'.

### Ashton

*(alt. Ashtyn)*

Old English, meaning 'ash tree town'.

### Asia

Name of the continent.

### Asma

*(alt. Asmara)*

Arabic, meaning 'high-standing'.

### Aspen

*(alt. Aspynn)*

Name of the tree. Also name of a city in the US.

### Assumpta

*(alt. Assunta)*

Italian, meaning 'raised up'.

### Asta

*(alt. Asteria, Astor, Astoria)*

Greek or Latin, meaning 'star-like'.

### Astrid

Old Norse, meaning 'beautiful like a God'.

### Atara

Hebrew, meaning 'diadem'.

### Athena

*(alt. Athenais)*

The Greek goddess of wisdom.

### Aubrey

*(alt. Aubree, Aubriana, Aubrie)*

French, meaning 'elf ruler'.

## Audrey

(alt. Audra, Audrie, Audrina, Audry)

English, meaning 'noble strength'.

## Augusta

(alt. August, Augustine)

Latin, meaning 'worthy of respect'.

## Aura

(alt. Aurea)

Greek or Latin, meaning either 'soft breeze' or 'gold'.

## Aurelia

(alt. Aurelie)

Latin, meaning gold.

## Aurora

(alt. Aurore)

In Roman mythology, Aurora was the goddess of sunrise.

## Austine

(alt. Austen, Austin)

Latin, meaning 'worthy of respect'.

## Autumn

Name of the season.

## Ava

(alt. Avia, Avie)

Latin, meaning 'like a bird'.

## Avalon

(alt. Avalyn, Aveline)

Celtic, meaning 'island of apples'.

## Axelle

Greek, meaning 'father of peace'.

## Aya

(alt. Ayah)

Hebrew, meaning 'bird'.

## Ayanna

(alt. Ayana)

American, meaning 'grace'.

## Ayesha

(alt. Aisha, Aysha)

Persian, meaning 'small one'.

## Azalea

Latin, meaning 'dry earth'.

**A**

### Azalia

Hebrew, meaning 'aided by God'.

### Aziza

Hebrew, meaning 'mighty', or Arabic meaning 'precious'.

### Azure

*(alt. Azaria)*

French, meaning 'sky-blue'.

## Popular French names for boys and girls

Adele
Alain
Alphonse
Belle
Fleur
Jacques
Marc
Mathieu
Paulette
Sabine

# B Girls' names

## Babette
(alt. Babe)

French version of
Barbara, Greek meaning
'foreign'.

## Bailey
(alt. Baeli, Bailee)

English, meaning 'law
enforcer'.

## Bambi
Shortened version of the Italian
Bambina, meaning 'child'.

## Barbara
(alt. Barb, Barbie, Barbra)

Greek, meaning 'foreign'.

## Basma
Arabic, meaning 'smile'.

## Bathsheba
Hebrew, meaning 'daughter of
the oath'.

## Bay
(alt. Baya)

Plant or geographical name.

## Beata
Latin, meaning 'blessed'.

## Beatrice
(alt. Beatrix, Beatriz, Bellatrix)

Latin, meaning 'bringer of
gladness'.

## Becky
(alt. Beccie, Beccy, Beckie)

Shortened form of Rebecca,
Hebrew meaning 'joined'.

B

## Literary names

Alice (*Alice in Wonderland*, Lewis Carroll)
Beth (*Little Women*, Louisa M. Alcott)
Cora (*Last of the Mohicans*, James Fenimore Cooper)
Eliza (*Pygmalion*, George Bernard Shaw)
Gwendolen (*The Importance of Being Earnest*, Oscar Wilde)
Hermione (Harry Potter series, J. K. Rowling)
Isabella (Twilight series, Stephenie Meyer)
Matilda (*Matilda*, Roald Dahl)
Miranda (*The Tempest*, William Shakespeare)
Wendy (*Peter Pan*, J. M. Barrie)

### Bee

Shortened form of Beatrice,
meaning 'bringer of gladness'.

### Belinda

*(alt. Belen, Belina)*

Contraction of Belle and Linda,
meaning 'beautiful'.

### Bell

Shortened form of Isabel,
meaning 'pledged to God'.

### Bella

Latin, meaning 'beautiful'.

### Belle

French, meaning 'beautiful'.

### Belva

Latin, meaning 'beautiful view'.

### Bénédicta

Latin, the feminine of Benedict,
meaning 'blessed'.

### Benita

*(alt. Bernita)*

Spanish, meaning 'blessed'.

### Bennie

Shortened version of Bénédicta
and Benita.

**B**

## Berit

*(alt. Beret)*

Scandinavian, meaning 'splendid' or 'gorgeous'.

## Bernadette

French, meaning 'courageous'.

## Bernadine

French, meaning 'courageous'.

## Bernice

*(alt. Berenice, Berniece, Burnice)*

Greek, meaning 'she who brings victory'.

## Bertha

*(alt. Berta, Berthe, Bertie)*

German, meaning 'bright'.

## Beryl

Greek, meaning 'pale, green gemstone'.

## Bess

*(alt. Bessie)*

Shortened form of Elizabeth, meaning 'consecrated to God'.

## Beth

Hebrew, meaning 'house'. Also shortened form of Elizabeth, meaning 'consecrated to God'.

## Bethany

*(alt. Bethan)*

Hebrew, referring to a geographical location.

## Bethel

Hebrew, meaning 'house of God'.

## Bettina

Spanish version of Elizabeth, meaning 'consecrated to God'.

## Betty

*(alt. Betsy, Bette, Bettie, Bettye)*

Shortened version of Elizabeth, meaning 'consecrated to God'.

## Beulah

Hebrew, meaning 'married'.

## Beverly

*(alt. Beverlee, Beverley)*

English, meaning 'beaver stream'.

B

### Beyoncé

American, made popular by
the singer.

### Bianca
(alt. Blanca)

Italian, meaning 'white'.

### Bijou

French, meaning 'precious
ring'.

### Billie
(alt. Bill, Billy, Billye)

Shortened version of
Wilhelmina, meaning
'determined'.

### Bina

Hebrew, meaning 'knowledge'.

### Birgit
(alt. Birgitta)

Norwegian, meaning
'splendid'.

### Blair

Scottish Gaelic, meaning 'flat,
plain area'.

### Blake
(alt. Blakely, Blakelyn)

English, meaning either 'pale-
skinned' or 'dark'.

### Blanche
(alt. Blanch)

French, meaning 'white or
pale'.

### Bliss

English, meaning 'intense
happiness'.

### Blithe

English, meaning 'joyous'.

### Blodwen

Welsh, meaning 'white flower'.

### Blossom

English, meaning 'flowerlike'.

### Blythe
(alt. Bly)

English, meaning 'happy and
carefree'.

### Bobbi
(alt. Bobbie, Bobby)

Shortened version of Roberta,
meaning 'bright fame'.

**B**

## Bonita

Spanish, meaning 'pretty'.

## Bonnie

*(alt. Bonny)*

Scottish, meaning 'fair of face'.

## Brandy

*(alt. Brandee, Brandi, Brandie)*

Name of the liquor.

## Brea

*(alt. Bree, Bria)*

Shortened form of Brianna, meaning 'strong'.

## Brenda

English, meaning 'burning or stinking hair'.

## Brianna

*(alt. Breana, Breann, Breanna, Breanne, Brenna, Brenyn, Briana, Brianne, Bryanna)*

Irish Gaelic, meaning 'strong'.

## Bridget

*(alt. Bridgett, Bridgette, Brigette, Brigid, Brigitta, Brigitte)*

Irish Gaelic, meaning 'strength and power'.

## Brier

French, meaning 'heather'.

## Brit

*(alt. Britt, Britta)*

Celtic, meaning 'spotted' or 'freckled'.

## Britannia

Latin, meaning 'Britain'.

## Brittany

*(alt. Britany, Britney, Britni, Brittani, Brittanie, Brittney, Brittni, Brittny)*

Latin, meaning 'from England'.

---

## Biblical names

Elizabeth
Eve
Hannah
Leah
Mary
Miriam
Rachel
Rebecca
Ruth
Sarah

---

B

## Bronwyn
*(alt. Bronwen)*

Welsh, meaning 'fair breast'.

## Brooke
*(alt. Brook)*

English, meaning 'small stream'.

## Brooklyn
*(alt. Brooklynn)*

Name of a New York borough.

## Brunhilda

German, meaning 'armor-wearing fighting maid'.

## Bryn
*(alt. Brynn)*

Welsh, meaning 'mount'.

## Bryony
*(alt. Briony)*

Name of a European vine.

## Popular Indian names for boys and girls

Ajay
Bharat
Deepal
Haresh
Jaya
Manisha
Paresh
Rabiya
Ravi
Sunita

# C Girls' names

## Cadence
Latin, meaning 'with rhythm'.

## Cai
Vietnamese, meaning 'feminine'.

## Caitlin
(alt. Cadyn, Caitlann, Caitlyn, Caitlynn)
Greek, meaning 'pure'.

## Calandra
Greek, meaning 'lark'.

## Calantha
(alt. Calanthe)
Greek, meaning 'lovely flower'.

## Caledonia
Latin, meaning 'from Scotland'.

## Calla
Greek, meaning 'beautiful'.

## Callie
(alt. Caleigh, Cali, Calleigh, Cally)
Greek, meaning 'beauty'.

## Calliope
Greek, meaning 'beautiful voice'. From the muse of epic poetry in Greek mythology.

## Callista
(alt. Callisto)
Greek, meaning 'most beautiful'.

## Camas

Native American, from the root and bulb of the same name.

## Cambria

Welsh, from the alternative name for Wales.

## Camden

*(alt. Camdyn)*

English, meaning 'winding valley'.

## Cameo

Italian, meaning 'skin'.

## Cameron

*(alt. Camryn)*

Scottish Gaelic, meaning 'bent nose'.

## Camilla

*(alt. Camelia, Camellia, Camila, Camillia)*

Latin, meaning 'spiritual serving girl'.

## Camille

Latin, meaning 'spiritual serving girl'.

## Candace

*(alt. Candice, Candis)*

Latin, meaning 'brilliant white'.

## Candida

Latin, meaning 'white'.

## Candra

Latin, meaning 'glowing'.

## Candy

*(alt. Candi)*

Shortened form of Candace, meaning 'brilliant white'.

## Caoimhe

Celtic, meaning 'gentleness'.

## Caprice

Italian, meaning 'ruled by whim'.

## Cara

Latin, meaning 'darling'.

## Caren

*(alt. Carin, Caron, Caryn)*

Greek, meaning 'pure'.

**C**

## Carey

*(alt. Cari, Carie, Carri, Carrie, Cary)*

Welsh, meaning 'near the castle'.

## Carina

*(alt. Corina)*

Italian, meaning 'dearest little one'.

## Carissa

*(alt. Carisa)*

Greek, meaning 'grace'.

## Carla

*(alt. Charla)*

Feminine of the Old Norse Carl, meaning 'free man'.

## Carlin

*(alt. Carleen, Carlene)*

Gaelic, meaning 'little champion'.

## Carlotta

*(alt. Carlota)*

Italian, meaning 'free man'.

## Carly

*(alt. Carlee, Carley, Carli, Carlie)*

Feminine of the German Charles, meaning 'man'.

## Carmel

*(alt. Carmela, Carmelita, Carmella)*

Hebrew, meaning 'garden'.

## Carmen

*(alt. Carma, Carmina)*

Latin, meaning 'song'.

## Carol

*(alt. Carole, Carrol, Carroll, Caryl)*

Shortened form of Caroline, meaning 'man'.

## Caroline

*(alt. Carolann, Carolina, Carolyn, Carolynn)*

German, meaning 'man'.

## Carrington

English, meaning 'Charles's town'.

## Carys

*(alt. Cerys)*

Welsh, meaning 'love'.

## Casey

*(alt. Casy, Casie)*

Irish Gaelic, meaning 'watchful'.

C

## Saints' names

Ada
Agatha
Catherine
Felicity
Helena
Joan
Lydia
Margaret
Mary
Teresa

### Cassandra
(alt. Casandra, Cassandre)
Greek, meaning 'one who prophesies doom'.

### Cassia
(alt. Casia, Casie, Cassie)
Greek, meaning 'cinnamon'.

### Cassidy
Irish, meaning 'clever'.

### Catalina
(alt. Catarina, Caterina)
Spanish version of Catherine, meaning 'pure'.

### Catherine
(alt. Catharine, Cathrine, Cathryn)
Greek, meaning 'pure'.

### Cathleen
Irish version of Catherine, meaning 'pure'.

### Cathy
(alt. Cathey, Cathi, Cathie)
Shortened form of Catherine, meaning 'pure'.

### Caty
(alt. Caddie, Caitee, Cate, Catie)
Shortened form of Catherine, meaning 'pure'.

### Cayley
(alt. Cayla, Caylee, Caylen)
American, meaning 'pure'.

### Cecile
(alt. Cecilie)
Latin, meaning 'blind one'.

### Cecilia
(alt. Cecelia, Cecily, Cicely, Cicily)
Latin, meaning 'blind one'.

**C**

## Celena

Greek, meaning 'goddess of the moon'.

## Celeste

(alt. Celestina, Celestine)

Latin, meaning 'heavenly'.

## Celine

(alt. Celia, Celina)

French version of Celeste, meaning 'heavenly'.

## Cerise

French, meaning 'cherry'.

## Chanah

Hebrew, meaning 'grace'.

## Chance

Middle English, meaning 'good fortune'.

## Chandler

(alt. Chandell)

English, meaning 'candle maker'.

## Chandra

(alt. Chanda, Chandry)

Sanskrit, meaning 'like the moon'.

## Chanel

(alt. Chanelle)

French, from the designer of the same name.

## Chantal

(alt. Chantel, Chantelle, Chantilly)

French, meaning 'stony spot'.

## Chardonnay

French, from the wine variety of the same name.

## Charis

(alt. Charice, Charissa, Charisse)

Greek, meaning 'grace'.

## Charity

Latin, meaning 'brotherly love'.

## Charlene

(alt. Charleen, Charline)

German, meaning 'man'.

## Charlie

(alt. Charlee, Charley, Charlize, Charly)

Shortened form of Charlotte, meaning 'little and feminine'.

C

## Charlotte
*(alt. Charnette, Charolette)*
French, meaning 'little and feminine'.

## Charmaine
Latin, meaning 'clan'.

## Chastity
Latin, meaning 'purity'.

## Chava
*(alt. Chaya)*
Hebrew, meaning 'beloved'.

## Chelsea
*(alt. Chelsee, Chelsey, Chelsi, Chelsie)*
English, meaning 'port or landing place'.

## Cher
French, meaning 'beloved'.

## Cherie
*(alt. Cheri, Cherise)*
French, meaning 'dear'.

## Cherish
*(alt. Cherith)*
English, meaning 'to treasure'.

## Chermona
Hebrew, meaning 'sacred mountain'.

## Cherry
*(alt. Cherri)*
French, meaning 'cherry fruit'.

---

## TV personality names

Cat (Deeley)
Connie (Chung)
Ellen (DeGeneres)
Giada (De Laurentiis)
Giuliana (Rancic)
Mary (Hart)
Oprah (Winfrey)
Padma (Lakshmi)
Samantha (Harris)
Tyra (Banks)

**C**

## Cheryl
(alt. Cheryle)

English, meaning 'little and womanly'.

## Chesney
English, meaning 'place to camp'.

## Cheyenne
(alt. Cheyanne)

Native American, from the tribe of the same name.

## Chiara
(alt. Ceara, Chiarina, Ciara)

Italian, meaning 'light'.

## China
From the country of the same name.

## Chiquita
Spanish, meaning 'little one'.

## Chloe
(alt. Cloe)

Greek, meaning 'pale green shoot'.

## Chloris
Greek, meaning 'pale'.

## Chris
(alt. Chrissy, Christa, Christie, Christy, Crissy, Cristy)

Shortened form of Christina, meaning 'anointed Christian'.

## Christabel
Latin and French, meaning 'fair Christian'.

## Christina
(alt. Christiana, Cristina)

Greek, meaning 'anointed Christian'.

## Christine
(alt. Christeen, Christen, Christene, Christian, Christiane, Christin)

Greek, meaning 'anointed Christian'.

## Chuma
Aramaic, meaning 'warmth'.

## Cierra
(alt. Ciera)

Irish, meaning 'black'.

## Cinderella
French, meaning 'little ash-girl'.

C

## Cindy
(alt. Cinda, Cindi, Cyndi)

Shortened form of Cynthia, meaning 'goddess from the mountain'.

## Cinnamon
Greek, from the spice of the same name.

## Citlali
(alt. Citlalli)

Aztec, meaning 'star'.

## Citrine
Latin, from the gemstone of the same name.

## Claire
(alt. Clare)

Latin, meaning 'bright'.

## Clara
(alt. Claira)

Latin, meaning 'bright'.

## Clarabelle
(alt. Claribel)

Contraction of Clara and Isobel, meaning 'bright' and 'consecrated to God'.

## Clarissa
(alt. Clarice, Clarisse)

Variation of Claire, meaning 'bright'.

## Clarity
Latin, meaning 'lucid'.

## Claudette
Latin, meaning 'lame'.

## Claudia
(alt. Claudie, Claudine)

Latin, meaning 'lame'.

## Clematis
Greek, meaning 'vine'.

## Clementine
(alt. Clemency, Clementina, Clemmie)

Latin, meaning 'mild and merciful'.

## Cleopatra
Greek, meaning 'her father's renown'.

## Clio
(alt. Cleo, Cliona)

Greek, from the muse of history of the same name.

C

## Clodagh

Irish, meaning 'river'.

## Clotilda

(alt. Clothilda, Clothilde, Clotilde)

German, meaning 'renowned battle'.

## Clover

English, from the flower of the same name.

## Coco

Spanish, meaning 'help'.

## Cody

English, meaning 'pillow'.

## Colleen

(alt. Coleen)

Irish Gaelic, meaning 'girl'.

## Collette

(alt. Colette)

Greek/French, meaning 'people of victory'.

## Connie

Latin, meaning 'steadfast'.

## Constance

(alt. Constanza)

Latin, meaning 'steadfast'.

## Consuelo

(alt. Consuela)

Spanish, meaning 'comfort'.

## Cora

Greek, meaning 'maiden'.

## Coral

(alt. Coralie, Coraline, Corelia, Corene)

Latin, from the marine life of the same name.

## Corazon

Spanish, meaning 'heart'.

## Cordelia

(alt. Cordia, Cordie)

Latin, meaning 'heart'.

## Corey

(alt. Cori, Corrie, Cory)

Irish Gaelic, meaning 'the hollow'.

## Corin

(alt. Corine)

Latin, meaning 'spear'.

## Corinne

(alt. Corinna, Corrine)

French version of Cora, meaning 'maiden'.

C

231

Corliss
English, meaning 'cheery'.

Cornelia
Latin, meaning 'like a horn'.

Cosette
French, meaning 'people of victory'.

Cosima
(alt. Cosmina)
Greek, meaning 'order'.

Courtney
(alt. Cortney)
English, meaning 'court-dweller'.

Creola
French, meaning 'American-born, English descent'.

Crescent
French, meaning 'increasing'.

Cressida
From the heroine in Greek mythology of the same name.

Crystal
(alt. Christal, Chrystal, Cristal)
Greek, meaning 'ice'.

Csilla
Hungarian, meaning 'defences'.

Cynara
Greek, meaning 'thistly plant'.

Cynthia
Greek, meaning 'goddess from the mountain'.

Cyra
Persian, meaning 'sun'.

Cyrilla
Latin, meaning 'lordly'.

C

# D Girls' names

### Dacey
Irish Gaelic, meaning 'from the south'.

### Dada
Nigerian, meaning 'curly haired'.

### Dagmar
German, meaning 'day's glory'.

### Dagny
Nordic, meaning 'new day'.

### Dahlia
Scandinavian, from the flower of the same name.

### Dai
Japanese, meaning 'great'.

### Daisy
*(alt. Dasia)*
English, meaning 'eye of the day'.

### Dakota
Native American, meaning 'allies'.

### Dalia
*(alt. Dalila)*
Hebrew, meaning 'delicate branch'.

### Dallas
Scottish Gaelic, from the village of the same name. Also a city in Texas.

### Damaris
Greek, meaning 'calf'.

233

## Damita

Spanish, meaning 'little noblewoman'.

## Dana

*(alt. Dania, Danna, Dayna)*

English, meaning 'from Denmark'.

## Danae

Greek, from the mythological heroine of the same name.

## Danica

*(alt. Danika)*

Latin, meaning 'from Denmark'.

## Danielle

*(alt. Danelle, Daniela, Daniella, Danila, Danyelle)*

The feminine form of the Hebrew Daniel, meaning 'God is my judge'.

## Danita

English, meaning 'God will judge'.

## Daphne

*(alt. Dafne, Daphna)*

Greek, meaning 'laurel tree'.

## Dara

Hebrew/Persian, meaning 'wisdom'.

## Darby

*(alt. Darbi, Darbie)*

Irish, meaning 'park with deer'.

## Darcie

*(alt. Darci, Darcy)*

Irish Gaelic, meaning 'dark'.

## Daria

Greek, meaning 'rich'.

## Darla

English, meaning 'darling'.

## Darlene

*(alt. Darleen, Darline)*

American, meaning 'darling'.

## Daryl

*(alt. Darryl)*

English, originally used as a last name.

## Davina

Hebrew, meaning 'loved one'.

## Dawn

*(alt. Dawna)*

English, meaning 'the dawn'.

**D**

## Daya

Hebrew, meaning 'bird of prey'.

## Deanna

*(alt. Dayana, Deana, Deanna, Deanne)*

English, meaning 'valley'.

## Debbie

*(alt. Debbi, Debby, Debi)*

Shortened form of Deborah, meaning 'bee'.

## Deborah

*(alt. Debbra, Debora, Debra, Debrah)*

Hebrew, meaning 'bee'.

## December

Latin, meaning 'tenth month'.

## Dee

Welsh, meaning 'swarthy'.

## Deidre

*(alt. Deidra, Deirdre)*

Irish, meaning 'raging woman'.

## Deja

*(alt. Dejah)*

French, meaning 'already'.

## Delaney

Irish Gaelic, meaning 'offspring of the challenger'.

## Delia

Greek, meaning 'from Delos'.

## Delilah

*(alt. Delina)*

Hebrew, meaning 'seductive'.

## Della

*(alt. Dell)*

Shortened form of Adele, meaning 'nobility'.

## Delores

*(alt. Deloris)*

Spanish, meaning 'sorrows'.

## Delphine

*(alt. Delpha, Delphia, Delphina, Delphinia)*

Greek, meaning 'dolphin'.

## Delta

Greek, meaning 'fourth child'.

## Demetria

*(alt. Demetrice, Dimitria)*

Greek, from the mythological heroine of the same name.

**D**

## Demi

French, meaning 'half'.

## Dena

*(alt. Deena)*

English, meaning 'from the valley'.

## Denise

*(alt. Denice, Denisa, Denisse)*

French, meaning 'follower of Dionysius'.

## Desdemona

Greek, meaning 'wretchedness'.

## Desiree

*(alt. Desirae)*

French, meaning 'much desired'.

## Desma

Greek, meaning 'blinding oath'.

## Destiny

*(alt. Destany, Destinee, Destiney, Destini)*

French, meaning 'fate'.

## Deva

Hindi, meaning 'God-like'.

## Devin

*(alt. Devinne)*

Irish Gaelic, meaning 'poet'.

## Devon

English, from the county of the same name.

## Diamond

English, meaning 'brilliant'.

## Diana

*(alt. Dian, Diane, Dianna, Dianne)*

Roman, meaning 'divine'.

## Diandra

Greek, meaning 'two males'.

## Dilys

Welsh, meaning 'reliable'.

## Dimona

Hebrew, meaning 'south'.

## Dinah

*(alt. Dina)*

Hebrew, meaning 'justified'.

## Dionne

Greek, from the mythological heroine of the same name.

D

## Uncommon three syllable names

| | |
|---|---|
| Annabel | India |
| Cassandra | Priscilla |
| Evelyn | Tamara |
| Gloria | Vanessa |
| Harriet | |

### Divine

Italian, meaning 'heavenly'.

### Dixie

French, meaning 'tenth'.

### Dodie

Hebrew, meaning 'well-loved'.

### Dolly

*(alt. Dollie)*

Shortened form of Dorothy, meaning 'gift of 'God'.

### Dolores

*(alt. Doloris)*

Spanish, meaning 'sorrows'.

### Dominique

*(alt. Domenica, Dominica, Domonique)*

Latin, meaning 'Lord'.

### Donata

Latin, meaning 'given'.

### Donna

*(alt. Dona, Donnie)*

Italian, meaning 'lady'.

### Dora

Greek, meaning 'gift'.

### Dorcas

Greek, meaning 'gazelle'.

### Doreen

*(alt. Dorene, Dorine)*

Irish Gaelic, meaning 'brooding'.

### Doris

*(alt. Dorris)*

Greek, from the place of the same name.

**D**

## Dorothy

(alt. Dorathy, Doretha, Dorotha, Dorothea, Dorthy)

Greek, meaning 'gift of God'.

## Dorrit

(alt. Dorit)

Greek, meaning 'gift of God'.

## Dory

(alt. Dori)

French, meaning 'gilded'.

## Dottie

(alt. Dotty)

Shortened form of Dorothy, meaning 'gift of God'.

## Dove

(alt. Dovie)

English, from the bird of the same name.

## Drew

Greek, meaning 'masculine'.

## Drusilla

(alt. Drucilla)

Latin, meaning 'of the Drusus clan'.

## Dulcie

(alt. Dulce, Dulcia)

Latin, meaning 'sweet'.

## Dusty

(alt. Dusti)

Old German, meaning 'brave warrior'.

**D**

# E Girls' names

**Earla**

English, meaning 'leader'.

**Eartha**

English, meaning 'earth'.

**Easter**

Egyptian, from the festival of the same name.

**Ebba**

English, meaning 'fortress of riches'.

**Ebony**
*(alt. Eboni)*

Latin, meaning 'deep, black wood'.

**Echo**

Greek, meaning 'reflected sound'. From the mythological nymph of the same name.

**Eda**
*(alt. Edda)*

English, meaning 'wealthy and happy'.

**Edelmira**

Spanish, meaning 'admired for nobility'.

**Eden**

Hebrew, meaning 'pleasure'.

**Edie**
*(alt. Eddie)*

Shortened form of Eden, meaning 'pleasure'.

### Edina

Scottish, meaning 'from Edinburgh'.

### Edith

*(alt. Edyth)*

English, meaning 'prosperity through battle'.

### Edna

Hebrew, meaning 'enjoyment'.

### Edrea

English, meaning 'wealthy and powerful'.

### Edwina

English, meaning 'wealthy friend'.

### Effie

Greek, meaning 'pleasant speech'.

### Eglantine

French, from the shrub of the same name.

### Eibhlín

Irish Gaelic, meaning 'shining and brilliant'.

### Eileen

Irish, meaning 'shining and brilliant'.

### Ekaterina

*(alt. Ekaterini)*

Slavic, meaning 'pure'.

### Elaine

*(alt. Elaina, Elayne)*

French, meaning 'bright, shining light'.

### Elba

Italian, from the island of the same name.

### Elberta

English, meaning 'high-born'.

### Eldora

Spanish, meaning 'covered with gold'.

### Eleanor

*(alt. Elana, Elanor, Eleanora, Eleanore, Elena, Eleni, Elenor, Elenora, Elina, Elinor, Elinore)*

Greek, meaning 'light'.

**E**

## Electra

*(alt. Elektra)*

Greek, meaning 'shining', also from the myth.

## Elfrida

*(alt. Elfrieda)*

English, meaning 'elf power'.

## Eliane

Hebrew, meaning 'Jehovah is God'.

## Elise

French, meaning 'my vow to God'.

## Elissa

*(alt. Elisa)*

French, meaning 'pledged to God'.

## Eliza

*(alt. Elisha)*

Hebrew, meaning 'pledged to God'.

## Elizabeth

*(alt. Elisabet, Elisabeth, Elizabella, Elsbeth, Elspeth)*

Hebrew, meaning 'pledged to God'.

## Elke

German, meaning 'nobility'.

## Ella

German, meaning 'completely'.

## Elle

*(alt. Ellie)*

French, meaning 'she'.

## Ellen

*(alt. Elin, Eline, Ellyn)*

Greek, meaning 'shining'.

## Ellice

*(alt. Elyse)*

Greek, meaning 'the Lord is God'.

## Elma

*(alt. Elna)*

Latin, meaning 'soul'.

## Elmira

Arabic, meaning 'aristocratic lady'.

## Elodie

French, meaning 'marsh flower'.

## Eloise

*(alt. Elois, Eloisa, Elouise)*

French, meaning 'renowned in battle'.

E

## Elsa
*(alt. Else, Elsie)*
Hebrew, meaning 'pledged to God'.

## Elula
Hebrew, meaning 'August'.

## Elva
Irish, meaning 'noble'.

## Elvina
English, meaning 'noble friend'.

## Elvira
*(alt. Elvera)*
Spanish, from the place of the same name.

## Ember
*(alt. Embry)*
English, meaning 'spark'.

## Emeline
German, meaning 'industrious'.

## Emerald
English, meaning 'green gemstone'.

## Emery
*(alt. Emory)*
German, meaning 'ruler of work'.

## Emilia
Latin, meaning 'rival, eager'.

## Emily
*(alt. Emelie, Emilee, Emilie, Emlyn)*
Latin, meaning 'rival, eager'.

## Emma
German, meaning 'embraces everything'.

## Emmanuelle
Hebrew, meaning 'God is among us'.

## Emmeline
*(alt. Emmelina)*
German, meaning 'embraces everything'.

## Emmy
*(alt. Emi, Emme, Emmie)*
German, meaning 'embraces everything'.

## Ena
Shortened form of Georgina, meaning 'farmer'.

## Enid
*(alt. Eneida)*
Welsh, meaning 'life spirit'.

E

## Enola

Native American, meaning 'solitary'.

## Enya

Irish Gaelic, meaning 'fire'.

## Erica

*(alt. Ericka, Erika)*

Scandinavian, meaning 'ruler forever'.

## Erin

*(alt. Eryn)*

Irish Gaelic, meaning 'from the isle to the west'.

## Eris

Greek, from the mythological heroine of the same name.

## Erlinda

Hebrew, meaning 'spirited'.

## Erma

German, meaning 'universal'.

## Ermine

French, meaning 'weasel'.

## Erna

English, meaning 'sincere'.

## Ernestine

*(alt. Ernestina)*

English, meaning 'sincere'.

## Esme

French, meaning 'esteemed'.

## Esmeralda

Spanish, meaning 'emerald'.

## Esperanza

Spanish, meaning 'hope'.

## Estelle

*(alt. Estela, Estell, Estella)*

French, meaning 'star'.

## Esther

*(alt. Esta, Ester, Etha, Ethna, Ethne)*

Persian, meaning 'star'.

## Eternity

Latin, meaning 'forever'.

## Ethel

*(alt. Ethyl)*

English, meaning 'noble'.

## Etta

*(alt. Etter, Ettie)*

Shortened form of Henrietta, meaning 'ruler of the house'.

**E**

**Eudora**
Greek, meaning 'generous gift'.

**Eugenia**
*(alt. Eugenie)*
Greek, meaning 'well born'.

**Eulalia**
*(alt. Eula, Eulah, Eulalie)*
Greek, meaning 'sweet-speaking'.

**Eunice**
Greek, meaning 'victorious'.

**Euphemia**
Greek, meaning ' favorable speech'.

**Eva**
Hebrew, meaning 'life'.

**Evadne**
Greek, meaning 'pleasing one'.

**Evangeline**
*(alt. Evangelina)*
Greek, meaning 'good news'.

**Evanthe**
Greek, meaning 'good flower'.

**Eve**
*(alt. Evie)*
Hebrew, meaning 'life'.

**Evelina**
*(alt. Evelia)*
German, meaning 'hazelnut'.

**Evelyn**
*(alt. Evalyn, Evelin, Eveline, Evelyne)*
German, meaning 'hazelnut'.

**Everly**
*(alt. Everleigh, Everley)*
English, meaning 'grazing meadow'.

**Evette**
French, meaning 'yew wood'.

**Evonne**
*(alt. Evon)*
French, meaning 'yew wood'.

**E**

# F

# Girls' names

## Fabia
(alt. Fabiana, Fabienne, Fabiola, Fabriana)
Latin, meaning 'from the Fabian clan'.

## Fabrizia
Italian, meaning 'works with hands'.

## Faith
English, meaning 'loyalty'.

## Faiza
Arabic, meaning 'victorious'.

## Fallon
Irish Gaelic, meaning 'descended from a ruler'.

## Fanny
(alt. Fannie)
Latin, meaning 'from France'.

## Farica
German, meaning 'peaceful ruler'.

## Farrah
English, meaning 'lovely and pleasant'.

## Fatima
Arabic, meaning 'baby's nurse'.

## Faustine
Latin, meaning 'fortunate'.

## Fawn
French, meaning 'young deer'.

### Fay
*(alt. Fae, Faye)*

French, meaning 'fairy'.

### Felicia
*(alt. Felecia, Felice, Felicita, Felisha)*

Latin, meaning 'lucky and happy'.

### Felicity
Latin, meaning 'fortunate'.

### Fenella
Irish Gaelic, meaning 'white shoulder'.

---

## Old name, new fashion?

Bella
Carolyn
Clara
Dorothy
Emmeline
Hazel
Matilda
Nora
Penelope
Rosalie

---

### Fenia
Scandinavian, from the mythological giantess of the same name.

### Fern
*(alt. Ferne, Ferrin)*

English, from the plant of the same name.

### Fernanda
German, meaning 'peace and courage'.

### Ffion
*(alt. Fion)*

Irish Gaelic, meaning 'fair and pale'.

### Fia
Italian, meaning 'flame'.

### Fifi
Hebrew, meaning 'Jehovah increases'.

### Filomena
Greek, meaning 'loved one'.

**F**

## Finlay

*(alt. Finley)*

Irish Gaelic, meaning 'fair-headed courageous one'.

## Finola

*(alt. Fionnula)*

Irish Gaelic, meaning 'fair shoulder'.

## Fiona

Irish Gaelic, meaning 'fair and pale'.

## Fiora

Irish Gaelic, meaning 'fair and pale'.

## Flanna

*(alt. Flannery)*

Irish Gaelic, meaning 'russet hair'.

## Flavia

Latin, meaning 'yellow hair'.

## Fleur

French, meaning 'flower'.

## Flo

*(alt. Florrie, Flossie, Floy)*

Shortened form of Florence, meaning 'in bloom'.

## Flora

Latin, meaning 'flower'.

## Florence

*(alt. Florencia, Florene, Florine)*

Latin, meaning 'in bloom'.

## Florida

Latin, meaning 'flowery'. Also a state in America.

## Fran

*(alt. Frankie, Frannie)*

Shortened form of Frances, meaning 'from France'.

## Frances

*(alt. Francine, Francis)*

Latin, meaning 'from France'.

## Francesca

*(alt. Franchesca, Francisca)*

Latin, meaning 'from France'.

**F**

### Freda
*(alt. Freida, Frida, Frieda)*

German, meaning 'peaceful'.

### Frederica

German, meaning 'peaceful ruler'.

### Fuchsia

German, from the flower of the same name.

## Names of First Ladies

Barbara (Bush)
Edith (Roosevelt)
Elizabeth (Ford)
Grace (Coolidge)
Hillary (Clinton)
Jacqueline (Kennedy)
Martha (Washington)
Mary (Lincoln)
Michelle (Obama)
Nancy (Reagan)

**F**

# G Girls' names

**Gabby**
*(alt. Gabbi)*
Shortened form of Gabrielle,
meaning 'heroine of God'.

**Gabrielle**
*(alt. Gabriel, Gabriela,*
*Gabriella)*
Hebrew, meaning 'heroine of
God'.

**Gaia**
*(alt. Gaea)*
Greek, meaning 'the earth'.

**Gail**
*(alt. Gale, Gayla, Gayle)*
Hebrew, meaning 'my father
rejoices'.

**Gala**
French, meaning 'festive
merrymaking'.

**Galiena**
German, meaning 'high one'.

**Galina**
Russian, meaning 'shining
brightly'.

**Garnet**
*(alt. Garnett)*
English, meaning 'red
gemstone'.

**Gay**
*(alt. Gaye)*
French, meaning 'glad and
lighthearted'.

G

## Gaynor

Welsh, meaning 'white and smooth'.

## Gemini

Greek, meaning 'twin'.

## Gemma

Italian, meaning 'precious stone'.

## Gene

Greek, meaning 'well born'.

## Genesis

Greek, meaning 'beginning'.

## Geneva
(alt. Genevra)

French, meaning 'juniper tree'.

## Genevieve

German, meaning 'white wave'.

## Genie

Shortened form of Genevieve, meaning 'white wave'.

## Georgette

French, meaning 'farmer'.

---

### Names from ancient Rome

Agrippina
Antonia
Claudia
Drusilla
Honorata
Hortensia
Narcissa
Romana
Tatiana
Valeria

---

## Georgia
(alt. Georgiana, Georgianna, Georgie)

Latin, meaning 'farmer'.

## Georgina
(alt. Georgene, Georgine, Giorgina)

Latin, meaning 'farmer'.

## Geraldine

German, meaning 'spear ruler'.

## Gerda

Nordic, meaning 'shelter'.

## Geri
*(alt. Gerri, Gerry)*
Shortened form of Geraldine, meaning 'spear ruler'.

## Germaine
French, meaning 'from Germany'.

## Gertie
Shortened form of Gertrude, meaning 'strength of a spear'.

## Gertrude
German, meaning 'strength of a spear'.

## Gia
*(alt. Ghia)*
Italian, meaning 'God is gracious'.

## Gianina
*(alt. Giana)*
Hebrew, meaning 'God's graciousness'.

## Gigi
*(alt. Giget)*
Shortened form of Georgina, meaning 'farmer'.

## Gilda
English, meaning 'gilded'.

## Gilia
Hebrew, meaning 'joy of the Lord'.

## Gillian
Latin, meaning 'youthful'.

## Gina
*(alt. Geena, Gena)*
Shortened form of Regina, meaning 'queen'.

## Ginger
Latin, from the root of the same name.

## Ginny
Shortened form of Virginia, meaning 'virgin'.

## Giovanna
Italian, meaning 'God is gracious'.

## Giselle
*(alt. Gisela, Gisele, Giselle, Gisselle)*
German, meaning 'pledge'.

**G**

Gita
*(alt. Geeta)*
Sanskrit, meaning 'song'.

Giulia
*(alt. Giuliana)*
Italian, meaning 'youthful'.

Gladys
*(alt. Gladyce)*
Welsh, meaning 'lame'.

Glenda
Welsh, meaning 'fair and good'.

Glenna
*(alt. Glennie)*
Irish Gaelic, meaning 'glen'.

Gloria
*(alt. Glory)*
Latin, meaning 'glory'.

Glynda
*(alt. Glinda)*
Welsh, meaning 'fair'.

Glynis
Welsh, meaning 'small glen'.

Golda
*(alt. Goldia, Goldie)*
English, meaning 'gold'.

Grace
*(alt. Graça, Gracie, Gracin, Grayce)*
Latin, meaning 'grace'.

Grainne
*(alt. Grania)*
Irish Gaelic, meaning 'love'.

Gratia
*(alt. Grasia)*
Latin, meaning 'blessing'.

Greer
*(alt. Grier)*
Latin, meaning 'alert and watchful'.

Gregoria
Latin, meaning 'alert'.

Greta
*(alt. Gretel)*
Greek, meaning 'pearl'.

G

## Gretchen

German, meaning 'pearl'.

## Griselda

*(alt. Griselle)*

German, meaning 'gray fighting maid'.

## Gudrun

Scandinavian, meaning 'battle'.

## Guinevere

Welsh, meaning 'white and smooth'.

## Gwen

Shortened form of Gwendolyn, meaning 'fair bow'.

## Gwenda

Welsh, meaning 'fair and good'.

## Gwendolyn

*(alt. Gwendolen, Gwenel)*

Welsh, meaning 'fair bow'.

## Gwyneth

*(alt. Gwynneth, Gwynyth)*

Welsh, meaning 'happiness'.

## Gwynn

*(alt. Gwyn)*

Welsh, meaning 'fair blessed'.

## Gypsy

English, meaning 'of the Roman tribe'.

# Names from ancient Greece

Alexandra
Apollonia
Corinna
Irene
Lysandra
Melaina
Pelagia
Sophia
Xenia
Zenobia

## Popular Irish names for boys and girls

| | |
|---|---|
| Aidan | Eileen |
| Aisling | Kieran |
| Connor | Liam |
| Declan | Niamh |
| Deidre | Siobhan |

# H Girls' names

## Hadassah
Hebrew, meaning 'myrtle tree'.

## Hadley
English, meaning 'heather meadow'.

## Hadria
Latin, meaning 'from Adria'.

## Hala
Arabic, meaning 'halo'.

## Haley
(alt. Hailee, Hailey, Hailie, Haleigh, Hali, Halie)
English, meaning 'hay meadow'.

## Halima
(alt. Halina)
Arabic, meaning 'gentle'.

## Hallie
(alt. Halle, Halley, Hallie)
German, meaning 'ruler of the home or estate'.

## Hannah
(alt. Haana, Hana, Hanna)
Hebrew, meaning 'grace'.

## Harley
(alt. Harlene)
English, meaning 'the long field'.

## Harlow
English, meaning 'army hill'.

255

## Harmony

Latin, meaning 'harmony'.

## Harper

English, meaning 'minstrel'.

## Harriet

*(alt. Harriett, Harriette)*

German, meaning 'ruler of the home or estate'.

## Hattie

Shortened form of Harriet, meaning 'ruler of the home or estate'.

## Haven

English, meaning 'a place of sanctuary'.

## Hayden

Old English, meaning 'hedged valley'.

## Hayley

*(alt. Haylee, Hayleigh, Haylie)*

English, meaning 'hay meadow'.

## Hazel

*(alt. Hazle)*

English, from the tree of the same name.

## Heather

English, from the flower of the same name.

## Heaven

English, meaning 'everlasting bliss'.

## Hedda

German, meaning 'warfare'.

## Hedwig

German, meaning 'warfare and strife'.

## Heidi

*(alt. Heidy)*

German, meaning 'nobility'.

## Helen

*(alt. Halen, Helena, Helene, Hellen)*

Greek, meaning 'light'.

## Names with positive meanings

Belle (Beautiful)
Blythe (Carefree)
Felicity (Happy)
Lakshmi (Good)
Lucy (Light)
Millicent (Brave)
Mira (Wonderful)
Rinah (Joyful)
Sunny (Sunshine)
Yoko (Positive)

### Helga

German, meaning 'holy and sacred'.

### Heloise

French, meaning 'renowned in war'.

### Henrietta

(alt. Henriette)

German, meaning 'ruler of the house'.

### Hephzibah

Hebrew, meaning 'my delight is in her'.

### Hera

Greek, meaning 'queen'.

### Hermia

(alt. Hermina, Hermine, Herminia)

Greek, meaning 'messenger'.

### Hermione

Greek, meaning 'earthly'.

### Hero

Greek, meaning 'brave one of the people'.

### Hertha

English, meaning 'earth'.

### Hesper

(alt. Hesperia)

Greek, meaning 'evening star'.

### Hester
(alt. Hestia)

Greek, meaning 'star'.

### Hilary
(alt. Hillary)

Greek, meaning 'cheerful and happy'.

### Hilda
(alt. Hildur)

German, meaning 'battle woman'.

### Hildegarde
(alt. Hildegard)

German, meaning 'battle stronghold'.

### Hildred

German, meaning 'battle counsellor'.

### Hilma

German, meaning 'helmet'.

### Hollis

English, meaning 'near the holly bushes'.

### Holly
(alt. Holli, Hollie)

English, from the tree of the same name.

### Honey

English, meaning 'honey'.

### Honor
(alt. Honour)

Latin, meaning 'woman of honor'.

### Honora
(alt. Honoria)

Latin, meaning 'woman of honor'.

### Hope

English, meaning 'hope'.

### Hortense
(alt. Hortencia, Hortensia)

Latin, meaning 'of the garden'.

### Hulda

German, meaning 'loved one'.

### Hyacinth

Greek, from the flower of the same name.

H

# I Girls' names

## Iantha
Greek, meaning 'purple flower'.

## Ida
English, meaning 'prosperous'.

## Idell
*(alt. Idella)*
English, meaning 'prosperous'.

## Idona
Nordic, meaning 'renewal'.

## Ignacia
Latin, meaning 'ardent'.

## Ila
French, meaning 'island'.

## Ilana
Hebrew, meaning 'tree'.

## Ilaria
Italian, meaning 'cheerful'.

## Ilene
American, meaning 'light'.

## Iliana
*(alt. Ileana)*
Greek, meaning 'Trojan'.

## Ilona
Hungarian, meaning 'light'.

## Ilsa
German, meaning 'pledged to God'.

## Ima

German, meaning 'embraces everything'.

## Iman

Arabic, meaning 'faith'.

## Imelda

German, meaning 'all-consuming fight'.

## Imogen

(alt. Imogene)

Latin, meaning 'last-born'.

## Ina

Latin, meaning 'to make feminine'.

## Inaya

Arabic, meaning 'taking care'.

## India

(alt. Indie)

Hindi, from the country of the same name.

## Indiana

Latin, meaning 'from India'.

## Indigo

Greek, meaning 'deep blue dye'.

## Indira

(alt. Inira)

Sanskrit, meaning 'beauty'.

## Inez

(alt. Ines)

Spanish, meaning 'pure'.

## Inga

(alt. Inge, Ingeborg, Inger)

Scandinavian, meaning 'guarded by Ing'.

## Ingrid

Scandinavian, meaning 'beautiful'.

## Io

(alt. Eye)

Greek, from the mythological heroine of the same name.

## Ioanna

Greek, meaning 'grace'.

## Iola

(alt. Iole)

Greek, meaning 'cloud of dawn'.

**I**

## Iolanthe
Greek, meaning 'violet flower'.

## Iona
Greek, from the island of the same name.

## Ione
Greek, meaning 'violet'.

## Iphigenia
Greek, meaning 'sacrifice'.

## Ira
*(alt. Iva)*
Hebrew, meaning 'watchful'.

## Irene
*(alt. Irelyn, Irena, Irina, Irini)*
Greek, meaning 'peace'.

## Iris
Greek, meaning 'rainbow'.

## Irma
German, meaning 'universal'.

## Isabel
*(alt. Isabela, Isabell, Isabella, Isabelle, Isobel, Izabella, Izabelle)*
Spanish, meaning 'pledged to God'.

## Isadora
Latin, meaning 'gift of Isis'.

## Ishana
Hindi, meaning 'desire'.

## Isis
Egyptian, from the goddess of the same name.

## Isla
*(alt. Isa, Isela, Isley)*
Scottish Gaelic, meaning 'river'.

## Isolde
Welsh, meaning 'fair lady'.

## Ivana
Slavic, meaning 'Jehovah is gracious'.

## Ivette
Variation of Yvette, meaning 'yew wood'.

## Ivonne
Variation of Yvonne, meaning 'yew wood'.

## Ivory
Latin, meaning 'white as elephant tusks'.

I

## Ivy

English, from the plant of the same name.

## Ixia

South African, from the flower of the same name.

## Boys' names for girls (female spellings)

Ashley
Billie
Casey
Charlie
Elliott
Geri
Jamie
Jordan
Leigh
Toni

**I**

# J Girls' names

## Jacinda
(alt. Jacinta)
Spanish, meaning 'hyacinth'.

## Jackie
(alt. Jacque, Jacqui)
Shortened form of Jacqueline, meaning 'he who supplants'.

## Jacqueline
(alt. Jacalyn, Jacklyn, Jaclyn, Jacquelin, Jacquelyn, Jacquline, Jaquelin, Jaqueline)
French, meaning 'he who supplants'.

## Jade
(alt. Jada, Jaida, Jayda, Jayde)
Spanish, meaning 'green stone'.

## Jaden
(alt. Jadyn, Jaiden, Jayden)
Contraction of Jade and Hayden, meaning 'green hedged valley'.

## Jael
Hebrew, meaning 'mountain goat'.

## Jaime
(alt. Jaima, Jaimie, Jami, Jamie)
Spanish, meaning 'he who supplants'.

## Jamila
Arabic, meaning 'lovely'.

## Jan
(alt. Jann, Janna)

Hebrew, meaning 'the Lord is gracious'.

## Jana
(alt. Jaana)

Hebrew, meaning 'the Lord is gracious'.

## Janae
(alt. Janay)

American, meaning 'the Lord is gracious'.

## Jane
(alt. Jayne)

Feminine form of the Hebrew John, meaning 'the Lord is gracious'.

## Janelle
(alt. Janel, Janell, Jenelle)

American, meaning 'the Lord is gracious'.

## Janet
(alt. Janette)

Scottish, meaning 'the Lord is gracious'.

## Janice
(alt. Janis)

American, meaning 'the Lord is gracious'.

## Janie
(alt. Janney, Jannie)

Shortened form of Janet, meaning 'the Lord is gracious'.

## Janine
(alt. Janeen)

English, meaning 'the Lord is gracious'.

## Janoah
(alt. Janiya, Janiyah)

Hebrew, meaning 'quiet and calm'.

## January
Latin, meaning 'the first month'.

## Jasmine
(alt. Jasmin, Jazim, Jazmine)

Persian, meaning 'jasmine flower'.

## Jay
Latin, meaning 'jaybird'.

**J**

## Jayna

Sanskrit, meaning 'bringer of victory'.

## Jean

*(alt. Jeane, Jeanne)*

Scottish, meaning 'the Lord is gracious'.

## Jeana

*(alt. Jeanna)*

Latin, meaning 'queen'.

## Jeanette

*(alt. Jeannette, Janette)*

French, meaning 'the Lord is gracious'.

## Jeanie

*(alt. Jeannie)*

Shortened form of Jeanette, meaning 'the Lord is gracious'.

## Jeanine

*(alt. Jeannine)*

Latin, meaning 'the Lord is gracious'.

## Jemima

Hebrew, meaning 'dove'.

## Jemma

Italian, meaning 'precious stone'.

## Jena

Arabic, meaning 'little bird'.

## Jenna

Hebrew, meaning 'the Lord is gracious'.

## Jennifer

*(alt. Jenifer)*

Welsh, meaning 'white and smooth'.

---

## Flower names

Daisy
Flora
Heather
Hyacinth
Iris
Lily
Poppy
Primrose
Rose
Violet

---

## Jenny
(alt. Jennie)

Shortened form of Jennifer, meaning 'white and smooth'.

## Jerrie
(alt. Jeri, Jerri, Jerrie, Jerry)

German, meaning 'spear ruler'.

## Jerusha

Hebrew, meaning 'married'.

## Jeryl

English, meaning 'spear ruler'.

## Jessa

Shortened form of Jessica, meaning 'He sees'.

## Jessamy
(alt. Jessame, Jessamine, Jessamyn)

Persian, meaning 'jasmine flower'.

## Jessica
(alt. Jesica, Jessika)

Hebrew, meaning 'He sees'.

## Jessie
(alt. Jesse, Jessi, Jessy)

Shortened form of Jessica, meaning 'He sees'.

## Jesusa

Spanish, meaning 'mother of the Lord'.

## Jette
(alt. Jetta, Jettie)

Danish, meaning 'black as coal'.

## Jewel
(alt. Jewell)

French, meaning 'delight'.

## Jezebel
(alt. Jezabel, Jezabelle)

Hebrew, meaning 'pure and virginal'.

## Jill

Latin, meaning 'youthful'.

## Jillian

Latin, meaning 'youthful'.

## Jimena

Spanish, meaning 'heard'.

**J**

### Jo
Shortened form of Joanna, meaning 'the Lord is gracious'.

### Joan
Hebrew, meaning 'the Lord is gracious'.

### Joanna
(alt. Joana, Joanie, Joann, Joanne, Johanna, Joni)
Hebrew, meaning 'the Lord is gracious'.

### Jocasta
Italian, meaning 'lighthearted'.

### Jocelyn
(alt. Jauslyn, Jocelyne, Joscelin, Joslyn)
German, meaning 'cheerful'.

### Jody
(alt. Jodee, Jodi, Jodie)
Shortened form of Judith, meaning 'Jewish'.

### Joelle
(alt. Joela)
Hebrew, meaning 'Jehovah is the Lord'.

### Joie
French, meaning 'joy'.

### Jolene
Contraction of Joanna and Darlene, meaning 'gracious darling'.

### Jolie
(alt. Joely)
French, meaning 'pretty'.

### Jordan
(alt. Jordana, Jordin, Jordyn)
Hebrew, meaning 'descend'.

### Josephine
(alt. Josefina, Josephina)
Hebrew, meaning 'Jehovah increases'.

### Josie
(alt. Joss, Jossie)
Shortened form of Josephine, meaning 'Jehovah increases'.

### Jovita
(alt. Jovie)
Latin, meaning 'made glad'.

### Joy
Latin, meaning 'joy'.

## Joyce
Latin, meaning 'joyous'.

## Juanita
*(alt. Juana)*
Spanish, meaning 'the Lord is gracious'.

## Judith
*(alt. Judit)*
Hebrew, meaning 'Jewish'.

## Judy
*(alt. Judi, Judie)*
Shortened form of Judith, Hebrew meaning 'Jewish'.

## Jules
French, meaning 'Jove's child'.

## Julia
Latin, meaning 'youthful'.

## Julianne
*(alt. Juliana, Juliann, Julianne)*
Latin, meaning 'youthful'.

## Julie
*(alt. Juli)*
Shortened form of Julia, meaning 'youthful'.

## Juliet
*(alt. Joliet, Juliette)*
Latin, meaning 'youthful'.

## June
*(alt. Juna)*
Latin, after the month of the same name.

## Juniper
Dutch, from the shrub of the same name.

## Juno
*(alt. Juneau)*
Latin, meaning 'queen of heaven'.

## Justice
English, meaning 'to deliver what is just'.

## Justine
*(alt. Justina)*
Latin, meaning 'fair and righteous'.

## Jørgina
Dutch, meaning 'farmer'.

**J**

# K Girls' names

### Kadenza
*(alt. Kadence)*
Latin, meaning 'with rhythm'.

### Kaitlin
*(alt. Kaitlyn)*
Greek, meaning 'pure'.

### Kala
*(alt. Kaela, Kaiala, Kaila)*
Sanskrit, meaning 'black one'.

### Kali
*(alt. Kailey, Kaleigh, Kaley, Kalie, Kalli, Kally, Kaylee, Kayleigh)*
Sanskrit, meaning 'black one'.

### Kalila
Arabic, meaning 'beloved'.

### Kalina
Slavic, meaning 'flower'.

### Kalliope
*(alt. Calliope)*
Greek, meaning 'beautiful voice'. From the muse of the same name.

### Kallista
Greek, meaning 'most beautiful'.

### Kama
Sanskrit, meaning 'love'.

### Kami
Japanese, meaning 'lord'.

### Kamilla
*(alt. Kamilah)*
Slavic, meaning 'serving girl'.

## Place names

Ailsa
Alexandria
Brittany
Eden
India
Lydia
Martinique
Normandie
Paris
Skye

**Kana**

Hawaiian, from the demi-god of the same name.

**Kandace**
*(alt. Kandice)*
Latin, meaning 'glowing white'.

**Kandy**
*(alt. Kandi)*
Shortened form of Kandace, meaning 'glowing white'.

**Kara**
Latin, meaning 'dear one'.

**Karen**
*(alt. Karan, Karin, Karina, Karon, Karren)*
Greek, meaning 'pure'.

**Kari**
*(alt. Karie, Karri, Karrie)*
Shortened form of Karen, meaning 'pure'.

**Karimah**
Arabic, meaning 'giving'.

**Karishma**
Sanskrit, meaning 'miracle'.

**Karla**
German, meaning 'man'.

**Karly**
*(alt. Karlee, Karley, Karli)*
German, meaning 'free man'.

**Karlyn**
German, meaning 'man'.

**Karma**
Hindi, meaning 'destiny'.

## Karol
*(alt. Karolina, Karolyn)*
Slavic, meaning 'little and womanly'.

## Kasey
*(alt. Kacey, Kaci, Kacie, Kacy, Kasie, Kassie)*
Irish Gaelic, meaning 'alert and watchful'.

## Kassandra
Greek, meaning 'she who entangles men'.

## Katarina
*(alt. Katarine, Katerina, Katharina)*
Greek, meaning 'pure'.

## Kate
*(alt. Kat, Katie, Kathi, Kathie, Kathy, Kati, Katy)*
Shortened form of Katherine, meaning 'pure'.

## Katelyn
*(alt. Katelin, Katelynn, Katlin, Katlyn)*
Greek, meaning 'pure'.

## Katherine
*(alt. Katharine, Kathrine, Kathryn)*
Greek, meaning 'pure'.

## Kathleen
*(alt. Kathlyn)*
Greek, meaning 'pure'.

## Katrina
*(alt. Katina)*
Greek, meaning 'pure'.

## Kay
*(alt. Kaye)*
Shortened form of Katherine, meaning 'pure'.

## Kaya
Sanskrit, meaning 'nature', or Turkish, meaning 'rock'.

## Kayla
*(alt. Kaylah)*
Greek, meaning 'pure'.

## Kayley
*(alt. Kayley, Kayli, Kaylin)*
American, meaning 'pure'.

## Keeley
*(alt. Keely)*
Irish, meaning 'battle maid'.

## Keila
Hebrew, meaning 'citadel'.

### Keira

Irish Gaelic, meaning 'dark'.

### Keisha

*(alt. Keesha)*

Arabic, meaning 'woman'.

### Kelis

American, meaning 'beautiful'.

### Kelly

*(alt. Keli, Kelley, Kelli, Kellie)*

Irish Gaelic, meaning 'battle maid'.

### Kelsey

*(alt. Kelcie Kelsea, Kelsi, Kelsie)*

English, meaning 'island'.

### Kendall

*(alt. Kendal)*

English, meaning 'the valley of the Kent'.

### Kendra

English, meaning 'knowing'.

### Kenna

Irish Gaelic, meaning 'handsome'.

### Kennedy

*(alt. Kenadee, Kennedi)*

Irish Gaelic, meaning 'helmet head'.

### Kenya

African, from the country of the same name.

### Kenzie

Shortened form of Mackenzie, meaning 'son of the wise ruler'.

### Kerensa

Cornish, meaning 'love'.

### Kerrigan

Irish, meaning 'black haired'.

### Kerry

*(alt. Keri, Kerri, Kerrie)*

Irish, from the county of the same name.

### Khadijah

*(alt. Khadejah)*

Arabic, meaning 'premature baby'.

### Kiana

*(alt. Kia, Kiana)*

American, meaning 'fibre'.

## Kiara
Italian, meaning 'light'.

## Kiki
Spanish, meaning 'home ruler'.

## Kim
Shortened form of Kimberly, from the town of the same name.

## Kimberly
*(alt. Kimberleigh, Kimberley)*
Old English, meaning 'royal forest'.

## Kingsley
*(alt. Kinsley)*
English, meaning 'king's meadow'.

## Kinsey
English, meaning 'king's victory'.

## Kira
Greek, meaning 'lady'.

## Kiri
Maori, meaning 'tree bark'.

---

# Long names

Alexandria
Bernadette
Christabelle
Constantine
Evangeline
Gabrielle
Henrietta
Jacqueline
Marguerite
Wilhelmina

---

## Kirsten
*(alt. Kirstin)*
Scandinavian, meaning 'Christian'.

## Kirstie
*(alt. Kirsty)*
Shortened form of Kirsten, meaning 'Christian'.

## Kitty
*(alt. Kittie)*
Shortened form of Katherine, meaning 'pure'.

## Kizzy
Hebrew, meaning the plant 'cassia'.

**K**

## Klara

Hungarian, meaning 'bright'.

## Komal

Hindi, meaning 'soft and tender'.

## Konstantina

Latin, meaning 'steadfast'.

## Kora

*(alt. Kori)*

Greek, meaning 'maiden'.

## Kris

*(alt. Krista, Kristi, Kristie, Kristy)*

Shortened form of Kristen, meaning 'Christian'.

## Kristen

*(alt. Kristan, Kristin, Kristine)*

Greek, meaning 'Christian'.

## Krystal

*(alt. Kristal, Kristel)*

Greek, meaning 'ice'.

## Kwanza

*(alt. Kwanzaa)*

African, meaning 'beginning'.

## Kyla

*(alt. Kya, Kylah, Kyle)*

Scottish, meaning 'narrow spit of land'.

## Kylie

*(alt. Kiley, Kylee)*

Irish Gaelic, meaning 'graceful'.

## Kyra

Greek, meaning 'lady'.

## Kyrie

Greek, meaning 'the Lord'.

## Short names

Bea
Bo
Fay
Jan
Jo
Kay
Kim
May
Mia
Val

# L Girls' names

## Lacey
(alt. Laci, Lacie, Lacy)

French, from the town of the same name.

## Ladonna
Italian, meaning 'lady'.

## Lady
English, meaning 'bread kneader'.

## Laila
(alt. Layla, Leila, Lela, Lelah, Lelia)

Arabic, meaning 'night'.

## Lainey
(alt. Laine, Laney)

French, meaning 'bright light'.

## Lakeisha
(alt. Lakeshia)

American, meaning 'woman'.

## Lakshmi
(alt. Laxmi)

Sanskrit, meaning 'good omen'.

## Lana
Greek, meaning 'light'.

## Lani
(alt. Lanie)

Hawaiian, meaning 'sky'.

## Lara
Latin, meaning 'famous'.

L

## Laraine

French, meaning 'from Lorraine'.

## Larissa

*(alt. Larisa)*

Greek, meaning 'light-hearted'.

## Lark

*(alt. Larkin)*

English, meaning 'playful songbird'.

## Larsen

Scandinavian, meaning 'son of Lars'.

## Latifa

Arabic, meaning 'gentle and pleasant'.

## Latika

*(alt. Lotika)*

Hindi, meaning 'a plant'.

## Latisha

Latin, meaning 'happiness'.

## Latona

*(alt. Latonia)*

Roman, from the mythological heroine of the same name.

## Latoya

Spanish, meaning 'victorious one'.

## Latrice

*(alt. Latricia)*

Latin, meaning 'noble'.

## Laura

Latin, meaning 'laurel'.

## Laurel

Latin, meaning 'laurel tree'.

## Lauren

*(alt. Lauran, Loren)*

Latin, meaning 'laurel'.

## Laveda

*(alt. Lavada)*

Latin, meaning 'cleansed'.

## Lavender

Latin, from the plant of the same name.

## Laverne

*(alt. Lavern, Laverna)*

Latin, from the goddess of the same name.

### Lavinia
*(alt. Lavina)*
Latin, meaning 'woman of Rome'.

### Lavonne
*(alt. Lavon)*
French, meaning 'yew wood'.

### Leah
*(alt. Lea, Leia)*
Hebrew, meaning 'weary'.

### Leandra
Greek, meaning 'lion man'.

### Leanne
*(alt. Leann, Leanna, Leeann)*
Contraction of Lee and Ann, meaning 'meadow grace'.

### Leda
Greek, meaning 'gladness'.

### Lee
*(alt. Leigh)*
English, meaning 'pasture or meadow'.

### Leilani
Hawaiian, meaning 'flower from heaven'.

---

## 'Bad girl' names

Delilah
Desdemona
Jezebel
Lilith
Pandora
Roxy
Salome
Scarlett
Tallulah
Trixie

---

### Leith
Scottish Gaelic, meaning 'broad river'.

### Lena
*(alt. Leena, Lina)*
Latin, meaning 'light'.

### Lenna
*(alt. Lennie)*
German, meaning 'lion's strength'.

### Lenore
*(alt. Lenora)*
Greek, meaning 'light'.

**L**

**Léonie**
*(alt. Leona, Leone)*
Latin, meaning 'lion'.

**Leonora**
*(alt. Leonor, Leonore)*
Greek, meaning 'light'.

**Leora**
Greek, meaning 'light'.

**Leslie**
*(alt. Leslee, Lesley)*
Scottish Gaelic, meaning 'the gray castle'.

**Leta**
Latin, meaning 'glad and joyful'.

**Letha**
Greek, meaning 'forgetfulness'.

**Letitia**
*(alt. Leticia, Lettice, Lettie)*
Latin, meaning 'joy and gladness'.

**Lexia**
*(alt. Lexi)*
Greek, meaning 'defender of mankind'.

**Lia**
Italian, meaning 'bringer of the gospel'.

**Liana**
French, meaning 'to twine around'.

**Libby**
*(alt. Libbie)*
Shortened form of Elizabeth, meaning 'pledged to God'.

**Liberty**
English, meaning 'freedom'.

**Lida**
Slavic, meaning 'loved by the people'.

**Liese**
*(alt. Liesel, Liesl)*
German, meaning 'pledged to God'.

**Lila**
*(alt. Lilah)*
Arabic, meaning 'night'.

**Lilac**
Latin, from the flower of the same name.

**L**

## Lilia

*(alt. Lilias)*

Scottish, meaning 'lily'.

## Lilith

Arabic, meaning 'ghost'.

## Lillian

*(alt. Lilian, Liliana, Lilla, Lillianna)*

Latin, meaning 'lily'.

## Lily

*(alt. Lillie, Lilly)*

Latin, from the flower of the same name.

## Linda

*(alt. Lynda)*

Spanish, meaning 'pretty'.

## Linden

*(alt. Lindie, Lindy)*

European, from the tree of the same name.

## Lindsay

*(alt. Lindsey, Linsey)*

English, meaning 'island of linden trees'.

## Linette

Welsh, meaning 'idol'.

## Linnea

*(alt. Linnae, Linny)*

Scandinavian, meaning 'lime or linden tree'.

## Liora

*(alt. Lior)*

Hebrew, meaning 'I have a light'.

## Lisa

*(alt. Leesa, Lise, Liza)*

Hebrew, meaning 'pledged to God'.

## Lissa

Greek, meaning 'bee'.

## Lissandra

*(alt. Lisandra)*

Greek, meaning 'man's defender'.

## Liv

Nordic, meaning 'defence'.

## Livia

Latin, meaning 'olive'.

L

## Great female singers

Adele (Adkins)
Aretha (Franklin)
Billie (Holiday)
Dionne (Warwick)
Dolly (Parton)
Ella (Fitzgerald)
Gladys (Knight)
Jennifer (Hudson)
Judy (Garland)
Nina (Simone)

### Liz
*(alt. Lizzie, Lizzy)*
Shortened form of Elizabeth, meaning 'pledged to God'.

### Logan
Irish Gaelic, meaning 'small hollow'.

### Lois
German, meaning 'renowned in battle'.

### Lola
Spanish, meaning 'sorrows'.

### Lolita
Spanish, meaning 'sorrows'.

### Lona
Latin, meaning 'lion'.

### Lora
Latin, meaning 'laurel'.

### Lorelei
*(alt. Loralai, Loralie)*
German, meaning 'dangerous rock'.

### Lorenza
Latin, meaning 'from Laurentium'.

### Loretta
*(alt. Loreto)*
Latin, meaning 'laurel'.

### Lori
*(alt. Laurie, Lorie, Lorri)*
Latin, meaning 'laurel'.

### Lorna
Scottish, from the place of the same name.

## Lorraine

(alt. Loraine)

French, meaning 'from Lorraine'.

## Lottie

(alt. Lotta, Lotte)

French, meaning 'little and womanly'.

## Lotus

Greek, meaning 'lotus flower'.

## Lou

(alt. Louie, Lue)

Shortened form of Louise, meaning 'renowned in battle'.

## Louise

(alt. Louisa, Luisa)

German, meaning 'renowned in battle'.

## Lourdes

French, from the town of the same name.

## Love

English, meaning 'love'.

## Lowri

Welsh, meaning 'crowned with laurels'.

## Luanne

(alt. Luann, Luanna)

German, meaning 'renowned in battle'.

## Lucia

(alt. Luciana)

Italian, meaning 'light'.

## Lucille

(alt. Lucile, Lucilla)

French, meaning 'light'.

## Lucinda

English, meaning 'light'.

## Lucretia

(alt. Lucrece)

Spanish, meaning 'light'.

## Lucy

(alt. Lucie)

Latin, meaning 'light'.

## Ludmilla

Slavic, meaning 'beloved of the people'.

## Luella

(alt. Lue)

English, meaning 'renowned in battle'.

L

## Lulu
*(alt. Lula)*

German, meaning 'renowned in battle'.

## Luna

Latin, meaning 'moon'.

## Lupita

Spanish, short form of Guadelupe. From the town of the same name.

## Luz

Spanish, meaning 'light'.

## Lydia
*(alt. Lidia)*

Greek, meaning 'from Lydia'.

## Lynn
*(alt. Lyn, Lynna, Lynne)*

Spanish, meaning 'pretty;
English, meaning 'waterfall'.

## Lyra

Latin, meaning 'lyre'.

---

### Tennis players

Anna (Kournikova)
Billie Jean (King)
Chris (Evert)
Margaret (Smith Court)
Maria (Sharapova)
Martina (Hingis/
    Navrátilová)
Monica (Seles)
Serena (Williams)
Steffi (Graf)
Venus (Williams)

---

**L**

# M Girls' names

**Mab**

Irish Gaelic, meaning 'joy'.

**Mabel**

*(alt. Mabelle, Mable)*

Latin, meaning 'loveable'.

**Macaria**

Spanish, meaning 'blessed'.

**Mackenzie**

*(alt. Mackenzy)*

Irish Gaelic, meaning 'son of the wise ruler'.

**Macy**

*(alt. Macey, Maci, Macie)*

French, meaning 'Matthew's estate'.

**Mada**

English, meaning 'from Magdala'.

**Madden**

*(alt. Maddyn)*

Irish, meaning 'little dog'.

**Maddie**

*(alt. Maddi, Maddie, Madie)*

Shortened form of Madeline, meaning 'from Magdala'.

**Madeline**

*(alt. Madaline, Madalyn, Madeleine, Madelyn, Madilyn)*

Greek, meaning 'from Magdala'.

**Madge**

Greek, meaning 'pearl'.

**Madhuri**

Hindi, meaning 'sweet girl'.

### Madison
(alt. Maddison, Madisen, Madisyn)
English, meaning 'son of the mighty warrior'.

### Madonna
Latin, meaning 'my lady'.

### Maeve
Irish Gaelic, meaning 'intoxicating'.

### Mafalda
Spanish, meaning 'battle-mighty'.

### Magali
Greek, meaning 'pearl'.

### Magdalene
(alt. Magdalen, Magdalena)
Greek, meaning 'from Magdala'.

### Maggie
Shortened form of Margaret, meaning 'pearl'.

### Magnolia
Latin, from the flower of the same name.

### Mahala
(alt. Mahalia)
Hebrew, meaning 'tender affection'.

### Maia
(alt. Maja)
Greek, meaning 'mother'.

### Maida
English, meaning 'maiden'.

### Maisie
(alt. Maisey, Maisy, Maizie, Masie, Mazie)
Greek, meaning 'pearl'.

### Malka
Hebrew, meaning 'queen'.

### Mallory
(alt. Malorie)
French, meaning 'unhappy'.

### Malvina
Gaelic, meaning 'smooth brow'.

### Mamie
(alt. Mammie)
Shortened form of Margaret, meaning 'pearl'.

**M**

## Mandy
*(alt. Mandie)*

Shortened form of Amanda, meaning 'much loved'.

## Manisha
Sanskrit, meaning 'desire'.

## Mansi
Hopi, meaning 'plucked flower'.

## Manuela
Spanish, meaning 'the Lord is among us'.

## Mara
Hebrew, meaning 'bitter'.

## Marcela
*(alt. Marceline, Marcella, Marcelle)*

Latin, meaning 'war-like'.

## Marcia
Latin, meaning 'war-like'.

## Marcy
*(alt. Marci, Marcie)*

Latin, meaning 'war-like'.

## Margaret
*(alt. Margarete, Margaretta, Margarette, Margret)*

Greek, meaning 'pearl'.

## Margery
*(alt. Marge, Margie, Margit, Margy)*

French, meaning 'pearl'.

## Margo
*(alt. Margot)*

French, meaning 'pearl'.

## Marguerite
*(alt. Margarita)*

French, meaning 'pearl'.

## Maria
*(alt. Mariah)*

Latin, meaning 'bitter'.

## Marian
*(alt. Mariam, Mariana, Marion)*

French, meaning 'bitter grace'.

## Marianne
*(alt. Mariann, Maryann, Maryanne)*

French, meaning 'bitter grace'.

### Maribel

American, meaning 'bitterly beautiful'.

### Marie

French, meaning 'bitter'.

### Mariel

*(alt. Mariela, Mariella)*

Dutch, meaning 'bitter'.

### Marietta

*(alt. Marieta)*

French, meaning 'bitter'.

### Marigold

English, from the flower of the same name.

### Marika

Dutch, meaning 'bitter'.

### Marilyn

*(alt. Marilee, Marilene, Marilynn)*

English, meaning 'bitter'.

### Marin

American, from the county of the same name.

### Marina

*(alt. Marine)*

Latin, meaning 'from the sea'.

### Mariposa

Spanish, meaning 'butterfly'.

### Maris

Latin, meaning 'of the sea'.

### Marisa

Latin, meaning 'of the sea'.

### Marisol

Spanish, meaning 'bitter sun'.

### Marissa

American, meaning 'of the sea'.

### Marjolaine

French, meaning 'marjoram'.

### Marjorie

*(alt. Marjory)*

French, meaning 'pearl'.

### Marla

Shortened form of Marlene, meaning 'bitter'.

**Marlene**
*(alt. Marlen, Marlena)*
Hebrew, meaning 'bitter'.

**Marley**
*(alt. Marlee)*
American, meaning 'bitter'.

**Marlo**
*(alt. Marlowe)*
American, meaning 'bitter'.

**Marseille**
French, from the city of the same name.

**Marsha**
English, meaning 'war-like'.

**Martha**
*(alt. Marta)*
Aramaic, meaning 'lady'.

**Martina**
Latin, meaning 'war-like'.

**Marvel**
French, meaning 'something to marvel at'.

**Mary**
Hebrew, meaning 'bitter'.

**Masada**
Hebrew, meaning 'foundation'.

**Matilda**
*(alt. Mathilda, Mathilde)*
German, meaning 'battle-mighty'.

**Mattea**
Hebrew, meaning 'gift of God'.

**Maude**
*(alt. Maud)*
German, meaning 'battle-mighty'.

**Maura**
Irish, meaning 'bitter'.

**Maureen**
*(alt. Maurine)*
Irish, meaning 'bitter'.

**Mavis**
French, meaning 'thrush'.

**M**

## Maxine
*(alt. Maxie)*
Latin, meaning 'greatest'.

## May
*(alt. Mae, Maya, Maye, Mayra)*
Hebrew, meaning 'gift of God'.
Also the month.

## Mckenna
*(alt. Mackenna)*
Irish Gaelic, meaning 'son of
the handsome one'.

## Mckenzie
*(alt. Mckenzy, Mikenzi)*
Irish Gaelic, meaning 'son of
the wise ruler'.

## Medea
*(alt. Meda)*
Greek, meaning 'ruling'.

## Meg
Shortened form of Margaret,
meaning 'pearl'.

## Megan
*(alt. Meagan, Meghan)*
Welsh, meaning 'pearl'.

## Mehitabel
Hebrew, meaning 'benefited
by God'.

## Mehri
Persian, meaning 'kind'.

## Melanie
*(alt. Melania, Melany, Melonie)*
Greek, meaning 'dark-skinned'.

## Melba
Australian, meaning 'from
Melbourne'.

## Melia
*(alt. Meliah)*
German, meaning 'industrious'.

## Melina
Greek, meaning 'honey'.

## Melinda
Latin, meaning 'honey'.

## Melisande
French, meaning 'bee'.

## Melissa
*(alt. Melisa, Mellissa)*
Greek, meaning 'bee'.

**Melody**
*(alt. Melodie)*
Greek, meaning 'song'.

**Melvina**
Celtic, meaning 'chieftain'.

**Menora**
Hebrew, meaning 'candlestick'.

**Mercedes**
Spanish, meaning 'mercies'.

**Mercy**
English, meaning 'mercy'.

**Meredith**
*(alt. Meridith)*
Welsh, meaning 'great ruler'.

**Merle**
French, meaning 'blackbird'.

**Merry**
English, meaning 'light-hearted'.

**Meryl**
*(alt. Merrill)*
Irish Gaelic, meaning 'sea-bright'.

**Meta**
German, meaning 'pearl'.

**Mia**
Italian, meaning 'mine'.

**Michaela**
*(alt. Makaela, Makaila, Makayla, Micaela, Mikaela, Mikaila, Mikala, Mikayla)*
Hebrew, meaning 'who is like the Lord'.

**Michelle**
*(alt. Machelle, Mechelle, Michaele, Michal, Michele)*
French, meaning 'who is like the Lord'.

**Mickey**
*(alt. Mickie)*
Shortened form of Michelle, meaning 'who is like the Lord'.

**Migdalia**
Greek, meaning 'from Magdala'.

**Mignon**
French, meaning 'cute'.

## Mika
*(alt. Micah)*
Hebrew, meaning 'who resembles God'.

## Milada
Czech, meaning 'my love'.

## Milagros
Spanish, meaning 'miracles'.

## Milan
Italian, from the city of the same name.

## Mildred
English, meaning 'gentle strength'.

## Milena
Czech, meaning 'love and warmth'.

## Miley
American, meaning 'smiley'.

## Millicent
German, meaning 'high-born power'.

## Millie
*(alt. Milly)*
Shortened form of Millicent, meaning 'high-born power'.

## Mimi
Italian, meaning 'bitter'.

## Popular song names

Billie Jean ("Billie Jean", Michael Jackson)
Caroline ("Sweet Caroline", Neil Diamond)
Delilah ("Delilah", Tom Jones)
Eileen ("Come on Eileen", Dexy's Midnight Runners)
Eleanor ("Eleanor Rigby", The Beatles)
Georgia ("Georgia on My Mind", Ray Charles)
Mary ("Proud Mary", Ike and Tina Turner)
Peggy Sue ("Peggy Sue", Buddy Holly)
Roxanne ("Roxanne", The Police)
Sally ("Mustang Sally", Wilson Pickett)

## Mina
(alt. Mena)

German, meaning 'love'.

## Mindy
(alt. Mindi)

Latin, meaning 'honey'.

## Minerva
Roman, from the goddess of the same name.

## Ming
Chinese, meaning 'bright'.

## Minna
German, meaning 'helmet'.

## Minnie
German, meaning 'helmet'.

## Mira
Latin, meaning 'admirable'.

## Mirabel
(alt. Mirabella, Mirabelle)

Latin, meaning 'wonderful'.

## Miranda
(alt. Meranda)

Latin, meaning 'admirable'.

## Mirella
(alt. Mireille, Mirela)

Latin, meaning 'admirable'.

## Miriam
Hebrew, meaning 'bitter'.

## Mirta
Spanish, meaning 'crown of thorns'.

## Missy
Shortened form of Melissa, meaning 'bee'.

## Misty
(alt. Misti)

English, meaning 'mist'.

## Mitzi
German, meaning 'bitter'.

## Miu
Japanese, meaning 'beautiful feather'.

## Moira
(alt. Maira)

Irish, meaning 'bitter'.

## Molly
(alt. Mollie)

American, meaning 'bitter'.

**M**

## Mona

Irish Gaelic, meaning 'aristocratic'.

## Monica

*(alt. Monika, Monique)*

Latin, meaning 'adviser'.

## Monroe

Gaelic, meaning 'mouth of the river Rotha'.

## Montserrat

*(alt. Monserrate)*

Spanish, from the town of the same name.

## Morag

Scottish, meaning 'star of the sea'.

## Morgan

*(alt. Morgann)*

Welsh, meaning 'great and bright'.

## Moriah

Hebrew, meaning 'the Lord is my teacher'.

## Morwenna

Welsh, meaning 'maiden'.

## Moselle

*(alt. Mozell, Mozella, Mozelle)*

Hebrew, meaning 'savior'.

## Mulan

Chinese, meaning 'wood orchid'.

## Muriel

Irish Gaelic, meaning 'sea-bright'.

## Mya

*(alt. Myah)*

Greek, meaning 'mother'.

## Myfanwy

Welsh, meaning 'my little lovely one'.

## Myra

Latin, meaning 'scented oil'.

## Myrna

*(alt. Mirna)*

Irish Gaelic, meaning 'tender and beloved'.

## Myrtle

Irish, from the shrub of the same name.

# N Girls' names

## Nadia
(alt. Nadya)
Russian, meaning 'hope'.

## Nadine
French, meaning 'hope'.

## Nahara
Aramaic, meaning 'light'.

## Naima
Arabic, meaning 'water nymph'.

## Nalani
Hawaiian, meaning 'serenity of the skies'.

## Nan
(alt. Nanna, Nannie)
Hebrew, meaning 'grace'.

## Nancy
(alt. Nanci, Nancie)
Hebrew, meaning 'grace'.

## Nanette
(alt. Nannette)
French, meaning 'grace'.

## Naomi
(alt. Naoma, Noemi)
Hebrew, meaning 'pleasant'.

## Narcissa
Greek, meaning 'daffodil'.

**Nastasia**

Greek, meaning 'resurrection'.

**Natalie**

(alt. Natalia, Natalya, Nathalie)

Latin, meaning 'birth day'.

**Natasha**

(alt. Natasa)

Russian, meaning 'birth day'.

**Neda**

English, meaning 'wealthy'.

**Nedra**

English, meaning 'underground'.

**Neema**

Swahili, meaning 'born of prosperity'.

**Neka**

Native American, meaning 'goose'.

**Nell**

(alt. Nelda, Nell, Nella, Nellie, Nelly)

Shortened form of Eleanor, meaning 'light'.

**Nemi**

Italian, from the lake of the same name.

**Neoma**

Greek, meaning 'new moon'.

**Nereida**

Spanish, meaning 'sea nymph'.

**Nerissa**

Greek, meaning 'sea nymph'.

**Nettie**

(alt. Neta)

Shortened form of Henrietta, meaning 'ruler of the house'.

**Neva**

Spanish, meaning 'snowy'.

**Nevaeh**

American, meaning 'heaven'.

**Niamh**

(alt. Neve)

Irish, meaning 'brightness'.

## Nicki
*(alt. Nicky, Nikki)*
Shortened form of Nicola, meaning 'victory of the people'.

## Nicola
Greek, meaning 'victory of the people'.

## Nicole
*(alt. Nichol, Nichole, Nicolette, Nicolle, Nikole)*
Greek, meaning 'victory of the people'.

## Nidia
Spanish, meaning 'graceful'.

## Nigella
Irish Gaelic, meaning 'champion'.

## Nikita
Greek, meaning 'unconquered'.

## Nila
Egyptian, meaning 'Nile'.

## Nilda
German, meaning 'battle woman'.

## Nina
Spanish, meaning 'girl'.

## Nissa
Hebrew, meaning 'sign'.

## Nita
Spanish, meaning 'gracious'.

## Nixie
German, meaning 'water sprite'.

## Noel
*(alt. Noelle)*
French, meaning 'Christmas'.

## Nola
Irish Gaelic, meaning 'white shoulder'.

## Nona
Latin, meaning 'ninth'.

## Nora
*(alt. Norah)*
Shortened form of Eleanor, meaning 'light'.

## Noreen
*(alt. Norine)*
Irish, meaning 'light'.

**N**

## Norma

Latin, meaning 'pattern'.

## Normandie

*(alt. Normandy)*

French, from the province of the same name.

## Novia

Latin, meaning 'new'.

## Nuala

Irish Gaelic, meaning 'white shoulder'.

## Nydia

Latin, meaning 'nest'.

## Nysa

*(alt. Nyssa)*

Greek, meaning 'ambition'.

---

# Names of goddesses

Aphrodite (Love: Greek)
Demeter (Harvest: Greek)
Eos (Dawn: Greek)
Isis (Life: Egyptian)
Kali (Death: Indian)
Lakshmi (Wealth: Indian)
Minerva (Wisdom: Roman)
Nephthys (Death: Egyptian)
Saraswati (Arts: Indian)
Vesta (Hearth: Roman)

**N**

# O Girls' names

### Oceana
*(alt. Ocean, Océane, Ocie)*
Greek, meaning 'ocean'.

### Octavia
Latin, meaning 'eighth'.

### Oda
*(alt. Odie)*
Shortened form of Odessa, meaning 'long voyage'.

### Odele
*(alt. Odell)*
English, meaning 'woad hill'.

### Odelia
Hebrew, meaning 'I will praise the Lord'.

### Odessa
Greek, meaning 'long voyage'.

### Odette
*(alt. Odetta)*
French, meaning 'wealthy'.

### Odile
*(alt. Odilia)*
French, meaning 'prospers in battle'.

### Odina
Feminine form of Odin, from the Nordic god of the same name meaning 'creative inspiration'.

### Odyssey
Greek, meaning 'long journey'.

## Oksana

Russian, meaning 'praise to God'.

## Ola
*(alt. Olie)*

Greek, meaning 'man's defender'.

## Olena
*(alt. Olene)*

Russian, meaning 'light'.

## Olga

Russian, meaning 'holy'.

## Olivia
*(alt. Olivev, Oliviana, Olivié)*

Latin, meaning 'olive'.

## Ollie

Shortened form of Olivia, meaning 'olive'.

## Olwen

Welsh, meaning 'white footprint'.

## Olympia
*(alt. Olimpia)*

Greek, meaning 'from Mount Olympus'.

## Oma
*(alt. Omie)*

Arabic, meaning 'leader'.

## Omyra

Latin, meaning 'scented oil'.

## Ona
*(alt. Onnie)*

Shortened form of Oneida, meaning 'long-awaited'.

## Oneida

Native American, meaning 'long awaited'.

## Onyx

Latin, meaning 'veined gem'.

## Oona

Irish, meaning 'unity'.

## Opal

Sanskrit, meaning 'gem'.

## Ophelia
*(alt. Ophélie)*

Greek, meaning 'help'.

## Oprah

Hebrew, meaning 'young deer'.

## Ora
Latin, meaning 'prayer'.

## Orabela
Latin, meaning 'prayer'.

## Oralie
*(alt. Oralia)*
French, meaning 'golden'.

## Orane
French, meaning 'rising'.

## Orchid
Greek, from the flower of the same name.

## Color names

Blanche
Coral
Ebony
Fawn
Hazel
Olive
Rose
Scarlett
Sienna
Violet

## Oriana
*(alt. Oriane)*
Latin, meaning 'dawning'.

## Orla
*(alt. Orlaith, Orly)*
Irish Gaelic, meaning 'golden lady'.

## Orlean
French, meaning 'plum'.

## Orsa
*(alt. Osia, Ossie)*
Latin, meaning 'bear'.

## Otthid
Greek, meaning 'prospers in battle'.

## Ottilie
*(alt. Ottie)*
French, meaning 'prospers in battle'.

## Ouida
French, meaning 'renowned in battle'.

## Ozette
Native American, from the village of the same name.

O

## Popular Scottish names for boys and girls

| | |
|---|---|
| Aileen | Mac |
| Alastair | Malcolm |
| Angus | Rhona |
| Fergus | Rossalyn |
| Isla | Saundra |

# P Girls' names

### Padma
Sanskrit, meaning 'lotus'.

### Paige
*(alt. Page)*
French, meaning 'serving boy'.

### Paisley
Scottish, from the town of the same name.

### Palma
*(alt. Palmira)*
Latin, meaning 'palm tree'.

### Paloma
Spanish, meaning 'dove'.

### Pam
Shortened form of Pamela, meaning 'all honey'.

### Pamela
*(alt. Pamala, Pamella)*
Greek, meaning 'all honey'.

### Pandora
Greek, meaning 'all gifted'.

### Pangiota
Greek, meaning 'all is holy'.

### Pansy
French, from the flower of the same name.

## Paradisa
*(alt. Paradis)*
Greek, meaning 'garden orchard'.

## Paris
*(alt. Parisa)*
Greek, from the mythological hero of the same name.

## Parker
English, meaning 'park keeper'.

## Parthenia
Greek, meaning 'virginal'.

## Parthenope
Greek, from the mythological Siren of the same name.

## Parvati
Sanskrit, meaning 'daughter of the mountain'.

## Pascale
French, meaning 'Easter'.

## Pat
*(alt. Patsy, Patti, Pattie, Patty)*
Shortened form of Patricia, meaning 'noble'.

## Patience
French, meaning 'the state of being patient'.

## Patricia
*(alt. Patrice)*
Latin, meaning 'noble'.

## Paula
Latin, meaning 'small'.

## Pauline
*(alt. Paulette, Paulina)*
Latin, meaning 'small'.

## Paxton
Latin, meaning 'peaceful town'.

## Paz
Spanish, meaning 'peace'.

## Pazia
Hebrew, meaning 'golden'.

## Peace
English, meaning 'peace'.

## Pearl
*(alt. Pearle, Pearlie, Perla)*
Latin, meaning 'pale gemstone'.

**P**

## Gem and precious stone names

Amber
Crystal
Diamond
Emerald
Garnet
Jade
Opal
Pearl
Ruby

### Peggy
*(alt. Peggie)*
Greek, meaning 'pearl'.

### Pelia
Hebrew, meaning 'marvel of God'.

### Penelope
Greek, meaning 'bobbin worker'.

### Penny
*(alt. Penni, Pennie)*
Greek, meaning 'bobbin worker'.

### Peony
Greek, from the flower of the same name.

### Perdita
Latin, meaning 'lost'.

### Peri
*(alt. Perri)*
Hebrew, meaning 'outcome'.

### Perry
French, meaning 'pear tree'.

### Persephone
Greek, meaning 'bringer of destruction'.

### Petra
*(alt. Petrina)*
Greek, meaning 'rock'.

### Petula
Latin, meaning 'to seek'.

### Petunia
Greek, from the flower of the same name.

Peyton
*(alt. Payton)*
Old English, meaning 'fighting-man's estate'.

Phaedra
Greek, meaning 'bright'.

Philippa
Greek, meaning 'horse lover'.

Philomena
*(alt. Philoma)*
Greek, meaning 'loved one'.

Phoebe
Greek, meaning 'shining and brilliant'.

Phoenix
Greek, meaning 'red as blood'.

Phyllida
Greek, meaning 'leafy bough'.

Phyllis
*(alt. Phillia, Phylis)*
Greek, meaning 'leafy bough'.

Pia
Latin, meaning 'pious'.

Pilar
Spanish, meaning 'pillar'.

Piper
English, meaning 'pipe player'.

## Spelling options

C vs K (Catherine or Katherine)
E vs I (Alex or Alix)
G vs J (Geri or Jerry)
N vs NE (Ann or Anne)
O vs OU (Honor or Honour)
S vs Z (Susie or Suzie)
Y vs IE (Carry or Carrie)

**P**

## Pippa

Shortened form of Philippa, meaning 'horse lover'.

## Plum

Latin, from the fruit of the same name.

## Polly

Hebrew, meaning 'bitter'.

## Pomona

Latin, meaning 'apple'.

## Poppy

Latin, from the flower of the same name.

## Portia

(alt. Porsha)

Latin, meaning 'from the Portia clan'.

## Posy

English, meaning 'small flower'.

## Precious

Latin, meaning 'of great worth'.

## Priela

Hebrew, meaning 'fruit of God'.

## Primrose

English, meaning 'first rose'.

## Princess

English, meaning 'daughter of the monarch'.

## Priscilla

(alt. Priscila)

Latin, meaning 'ancient'.

## Priya

Hindi, meaning 'loved one'.

## Prudence

Latin, meaning 'caution'.

## Prudie

Shortened form of Prudence, meaning 'caution'.

## Prunella

Latin, meaning 'small plum'.

## Psyche

Greek, meaning 'breath'.

## Popular names of English and Scottish Queens and Consorts

| | |
|---|---|
| Anna | Mairi |
| Anne | Margaret |
| Catherine | Mary |
| Eleanor | Matilda |
| Elizabeth | Victoria |

**P**

# Q

# Girls' names

## Qiturah
Arabic, meaning 'incense'.

## Queen
*(alt. Queenie)*
English, meaning 'queen'.

## Quiana
American, meaning 'silky'.

## Quincy
*(alt. Quincey)*
French, meaning 'estate of the fifth son'.

## Quinn
Irish Gaelic, meaning 'counsel'.

## Foreign alternatives

Eleanor (Elenora, Elinor)
Helen (Galina, Helene)
Georgina (Jørgina)
Margaret (Gretel, Marguerite, Marjorie)
Sarah (Sara, Sarine, Zara)
Violet (Iolanthe)

## No-nickname names

| | |
|---|---|
| April | Jude |
| Beth | June |
| Dana | Karen |
| Joy | May |

# R Girls' names

**Rachel**
(alt. Rachael, Rachelle)
Hebrew, meaning 'ewe'.

**Radhika**
Sanskrit, meaning 'prosperous'.

**Rae**
(alt. Ray)
Shortened form of Rachel,
meaning 'ewe'.

**Rahima**
Arabic, meaning
'compassionate'.

**Raina**
(alt. Rain, Raine, Rainey, Rayne)
Latin, meaning 'queen'.

**Raissa**
(alt. Raisa)
Yiddish, meaning 'rose'.

**Raleigh**
(alt. Rayleigh)
English, meaning 'meadow of
roe deer'.

**Rama**
(alt. Ramey, Ramya)
Hebrew, meaning 'exalted'.

**Ramona**
(alt. Romona)
Spanish, meaning 'wise
guardian'.

## Rana
(alt. Rania, Rayna)

Arabic, meaning 'beautiful thing'.

## Randy
(alt. Randi)

Shortened form of Miranda, meaning 'admirable'.

## Rani
Sanskrit, meaning 'queen'.

## Raphaela
(alt. Rafaela, Raffaella)

Spanish, meaning 'healing God'.

## Raquel
(alt. Racquel)

Hebrew, meaning 'ewe'.

## Rashida
Turkish, meaning 'righteous'.

## Raven
(alt. Ravyn)

English, from the bird of the same name.

## Razia
Arabic, meaning 'contented'.

## Reagan
(alt. Reagen, Regan)

Irish Gaelic, meaning 'descendant of Riagán'.

## Reba
Shortened form of Rebecca, meaning 'joined'.

## Rebecca
(alt. Rebekah)

Hebrew, meaning 'joined'.

## Reese
(alt. Reece)

Welsh, meaning 'fiery and zealous'.

## Regina
Latin, meaning 'queen'.

## Reina
(alt. Reyna, Rheyna)

Spanish, meaning 'queen'.

## Rena
(alt. Reena)

Hebrew, meaning 'serene'.

## Renata
Latin, meaning 'reborn'.

**R**

**Rene**

Greek, meaning 'peace'.

**Renée**

*(alt. Renae)*

French, meaning 'reborn'.

**Renita**

Latin, meaning 'resistant'.

**Reshma**

*(alt. Resha)*

Sanskrit, meaning 'silk'.

**Reta**

*(alt. Retha, Retta)*

Shortened form of Margaret, meaning 'pearl'.

**Rhea**

Greek, meaning 'earth'.

**Rheta**

Greek, meaning 'eloquent speaker'.

**Rhiannon**

*(alt. Reanna, Rhian, Rhianna)*

Welsh, meaning 'witch'.

**Rhoda**

Greek, meaning 'rose'.

**Rhona**

Nordic, meaning 'rough island'.

**Rhonda**

*(alt. Ronda)*

Welsh, meaning 'noisy'.

**Ría**

*(alt. Rie, Riya)*

Shortened form of Victoria, meaning 'victor'.

**Ricki**

*(alt. Rieko, Rika, Rikki)*

Shortened form of Frederica, meaning 'peaceful ruler'.

**Riley**

Irish Gaelic, meaning 'courageous'.

**Rilla**

German, meaning 'small brook'.

**Rima**

Arabic, meaning 'antelope'.

R

## Riona

Irish Gaelic, meaning 'like a queen'.

## Ripley

English, meaning 'shouting man's meadow'.

## Risa

Latin, meaning 'laughter'.

## Rita

Shortened form of Margaret, meaning 'pearl'.

## River

*(alt. Riviera)*

English, from the body of water of the same name.

## Robbie

*(alt. Robi, Roby)*

Shortened form of Roberta, meaning 'bright fame'.

## Roberta

English, meaning 'bright fame'.

## Robin

*(alt. Robbin, Robyn)*

English, meaning 'bright flame'.

## Rochelle

*(alt. Richelle, Rochel)*

French, meaning 'little rock'.

## Rogue

French, meaning 'beggar'.

## Rohina

*(alt. Rohini)*

Sanskrit, meaning 'sandalwood'.

## Roisin

Irish Gaelic, meaning 'little rose'.

## Rolanda

German, meaning 'famous land'.

## Roma

Italian, meaning 'Rome'.

## Romaine

*(alt. Romina)*

French, meaning 'from Rome'.

## Romola

*(alt. Romilda, Romily)*

Latin, meaning 'Roman woman'.

R

## 'Powerful' names

Allura
Aubrey
Inga
Isis
Lenna
Ulrika

### Romy

Shortened form of Rosemary, meaning 'dew of the sea'.

### Rona

*(alt. Ronia, Ronja, Ronna)*

Nordic, meaning 'rough island'.

### Ronnie

*(alt. Roni)*

English, meaning 'strong counsel'.

### Rosa

Italian, meaning 'rose'.

### Rosabel

*(alt. Rosabella)*

Contraction of Rose and Belle, meaning 'beautiful rose'.

### Rosalie

*(alt. Rosale, Rosalia, Rosalina)*

French, meaning 'rose garden'.

### Rosalind

*(alt. Rosalinda)*

Spanish, meaning 'pretty rose'.

### Rosalyn

*(alt. Rosaleen, Rosaline, Roselyn)*

Contraction of Rose and Lynn, meaning 'pretty rose'.

### Rosamond

*(alt. Rosamund)*

German, meaning 'renowned protector'.

### Rose

Latin, from the flower of the same name.

### Roseanne

*(alt. Rosana, Rosanna, Rosanne, Roseann, Roseanna)*

Contraction of Rose and Anne, meaning 'graceful rose'.

### Rosemary

*(alt. Rosemarie)*

Latin, meaning 'dew of the sea'.

## Rosie
*(alt. Rosia)*

Shortened form of Rosemary, meaning 'dew of the sea'.

## Rosita

Spanish, meaning 'rose'.

## Rowena
*(alt. Rowan)*

Welsh, meaning 'slender and fair'.

## Roxanne
*(alt. Roxana, Roxane, Roxanna)*

Persian, meaning 'dawn'.

## Roxie

Shortened form of Roxanne, meaning 'dawn'.

## Rubena
*(alt. Rubina)*

Hebrew, meaning 'behold, a son'.

## Ruby
*(alt. Rubi, Rubie)*

English, meaning 'red gemstone'.

## Ruth
*(alt. Ruthe, Ruthie)*

Hebrew, meaning 'friend and companion'.

## Popular South American names for boys and girls

Atl
Centehua
Citlali
Coatl
Eréndira
Itzli
Matlal
Teiuc
Xochitl
Zolin

R

# S Girls' names

## Saba
*(alt. Sabah)*
Greek, meaning 'from Sheba'.

## Sabina
*(alt. Sabine)*
Latin, meaning 'from the Sabine tribe'.

## Sabrina
Latin, meaning 'the River Severn'.

## Sadie
*(alt. Sade, Sadye)*
Hebrew, meaning 'princess'.

## Saffron
English, from the spice of the same name.

## Safiya
Arabic, meaning 'sincere friend'.

## Sage
*(alt. Saga, Saige)*
Latin, meaning 'wise and healthy'.

## Sahara
Arabic, meaning 'desert'.

## Sakura
Japanese, meaning 'cherry blossom'.

## Sally
*(alt. Sallie)*
Hebrew, meaning 'princess'.

## Salome
*(alt. Salma)*
Hebrew, meaning 'peace'.

## Sam
*(alt. Sammie, Sammy)*
Shortened form of Samantha, meaning 'told by God'.

## Samantha
Hebrew, meaning 'told by God'.

## Samara
*(alt. Samaria, Samira)*
Hebrew, meaning 'under God's rule'.

## Sanaa
Arabic, meaning 'brilliance'.

## Sandra
*(alt. Saundra)*
Shortened form of Alexandra, meaning 'defender of mankind'.

## Sandy
*(alt. Sandi)*
Shortened form of Sandra, meaning 'defender of mankind'.

## Sangeeta
Hindi, meaning 'musical'.

## Sanna
*(alt. Saniya, Sanne, Sanni)*
Hebrew, meaning 'lily'.

## Santana
*(alt. Santina)*
Spanish, meaning 'holy'.

## Sapphire
*(alt. Saphira)*
Hebrew, meaning 'blue gemstone'.

## Sarah
*(alt. Sara, Sarai, Sariah)*
Hebrew, meaning 'princess'.

## Sasha
*(alt. Sacha, Sascha)*
Russian, meaning 'man's defender'.

## Saskia
*(alt. Saskie)*
Dutch, meaning 'the Saxon people'.

S

## Savannah
(alt. Savanah, Savanna, Savina)
Spanish, meaning 'treeless'.

## Scarlett
(alt. Scarlet)
English, meaning 'scarlet'.

## Scout
French, meaning 'to listen'.

## Sedona
(alt. Sedonia, Sedna)
Spanish, from the city of the same name.

## Selah
(alt Sela)
Hebrew, meaning 'cliff'.

## Selby
English, meaning 'manor village'.

## Selena
(alt. Salena, Salima, Salina, Selene, Selina)
Greek, meaning 'moon goddess'.

## Selma
German, meaning 'Godly helmet'.

## Seneca
Native American, meaning 'from the Seneca tribe'.

## Sephora
Hebrew, meaning 'bird'.

## September
Latin, meaning 'seventh month'.

## Seraphina
(alt. Serafina, Seraphia, Seraphine)
Hebrew, meaning 'ardent'.

## Serena
(alt. Sarina, Sereana)
Latin, meaning 'tranquil'.

## Serenity
Latin, meaning 'serene'.

## Shania
(alt. Shaina, Shana, Shaniya)
Hebrew, meaning 'beautiful'.

S

### Shanice

American, meaning 'from Africa'.

### Shaniqua

(alt. Shanika)

African, meaning 'warrior princess'.

### Shanna

English, meaning 'old'.

### Shannon

(alt. Shannan, Shanon)

Irish Gaelic, meaning 'old and ancient'.

### Shantal

(alt. Shantel, Shantell)

French, from the place of the same name.

### Shanti

Hindi, meaning 'peaceful'.

### Sharlene

German, meaning 'man'.

### Sharon

(alt. Sharen, Sharona, Sharron)

Hebrew, meaning 'a plain'.

---

## Spring names

April
Cerelia
Kelda
May
Primavera
Verda
Verna

---

### Shasta

American, from the mountain of the same name.

### Shauna

(alt. Shawna)

Irish, meaning 'the Lord is gracious'.

### Shayla

(alt. Shaylie, Shayna, Sheyla)

Irish, meaning 'blind'.

### Shea

Irish Gaelic, meaning 'from the fairy fort'.

### Sheena

Irish, meaning 'the Lord is gracious'.

S

## Sheila

(alt. Shelia)

Irish, meaning 'blind'.

## Shelby

(alt. Shelba, Shelbie)

English, meaning 'estate on the ledge'.

## Shelley

(alt. Shellie, Shelly)

English, meaning 'meadow on the ledge'.

## Shenandoah

Native American, meaning 'after an Oneida chief'.

## Sheridan

Irish Gaelic, meaning 'wild man'.

## Sherry

(alt. Sheri, Sherie, Sherri, Sherrie)

Shortened form of Cheryl, meaning 'man'.

## Sheryl

(alt. Sherryl)

German, meaning 'man'.

## Shiloh

Hebrew, meaning 'his gift'. From the Biblical place of the same name.

## Shirley

(alt. Shirlee)

English, meaning 'bright meadow'.

## Shivani

Sanskrit, meaning 'wife of Shiva'.

## Shona

Irish Gaelic, meaning 'God is gracious'.

## Shoshana

(alt. Shoshanna)

Hebrew, meaning 'lily'.

## Shura

Russian, meaning 'man's defender'.

## Sian

(alt. Sianna)

Welsh, meaning 'the Lord is gracious'.

S

## Sibyl
*(alt. Sybil)*

Greek, meaning 'seer and oracle'.

## Sidney
*(alt. Sydney)*

English, meaning 'from St Denis'.

## Sidonie
*(alt. Sidonia, Sidony)*

Latin, meaning 'from Sidonia'.

## Siena
*(alt. Sienna)*

Latin, from the town of the same name.

## Sierra

Spanish, meaning 'saw'.

## Signa
*(alt. Signe)*

Scandinavian, meaning 'victory'.

## Sigrid

Nordic, meaning 'fair victory'.

## Silja

Scandinavian, meaning 'blind'.

## Simcha

Hebrew, meaning 'joy'.

## Simone
*(alt. Simona)*

Hebrew, meaning 'listening intently'.

## Sinead

Irish, meaning 'the Lord is gracious'.

## Siobhan

Irish, meaning 'the Lord is gracious'.

## Siren
*(alt. Sirena)*

Greek, meaning 'entangler'.

## Siria

Spanish, meaning 'glowing'.

## Skye
*(alt. Sky)*

Scottish, from the island of the same name.

## Skyler
*(alt. Skyla, Skylar)*

Dutch, meaning 'giving shelter'.

## Sloane
(alt. Sloan)

Irish Gaelic, meaning 'man of arms'.

## Socorro
Spanish, meaning 'to aid'.

## Sojourner
English, meaning 'temporary stay'.

## Solana
Spanish, meaning 'sunlight'.

## Solange
French, meaning 'with dignity'.

## Soledad
Spanish, meaning 'solitude'.

## Soleil
French, meaning 'sun'.

## Solveig
Scandinavian, meaning 'woman of the house'.

## Sonia
(alt. Sonja, Sonya)

Greek, meaning 'wisdom'.

## Sophia
(alt. Sofia, Sofie, Sophie)

Greek, meaning 'wisdom'.

## Sophronia
Greek, meaning 'sensible'.

## Soraya
Persian, meaning 'princess'.

## Sorcha
Irish Gaelic, meaning 'bright and shining'.

## Sorrel
English, from the herb of the same name.

## Stacey
(alt. Stacie, Stacy)

Greek, meaning 'resurrection'.

## Star
(alt. Starla, Starr)

English, meaning 'star'.

## Stella
Latin, meaning 'star'.

S

## Stephanie
*(alt. Stefanie, Stephani, Stephany)*
Greek, meaning 'crowned'.

## Sue
*(alt. Susie, Suzy)*
Shortened form of Susan, meaning 'lily'.

## Sukey
*(alt. Sukey, Sukie)*
Shortened form of Susan, meaning 'lily'.

## Sula
American, meaning 'peace' or 'little she-bear'.

## Summer
English, from the season of the same name.

## Sunday
English, meaning 'the first day'.

## Sunny
*(alt. Sun)*
English, meaning 'of a pleasant temperament'.

## Suri
Persian, meaning 'red rose'.

## Surya
Hindi, from the god of the same name.

## Susan
*(alt. Susann, Suzan)*
Hebrew, meaning 'lily'.

## Susannah
*(alt. Susanna, Susanne, Suzanna, Suzanne)*
Hebrew, meaning 'lily'.

## Svetlana
Russian, meaning 'star'.

## Swanhild
Saxon, meaning 'battle swan'.

## Sylvia
*(alt. Silvia, Sylvie)*
Latin, meaning 'from the forest'.

---

## Summer names

August
June
Natsumi
Persephone
Soleil
Summer
Suvi

---

**S**

# T Girls' names

**Tabitha**
*(alt. Tabatha)*
Aramaic, meaning 'gazelle'.

**Tahira**
Arabic, meaning 'virginal'.

**Tai**
Chinese, meaning 'big'.

**Taima**
*(alt. Taina)*
Native American, meaning 'peal of thunder'.

**Talia**
*(alt. Tali)*
Hebrew, meaning 'heaven's dew'.

**Taliesin**
Welsh, meaning 'shining brow'.

**Talise**
*(alt. Talyse)*
Native American, meaning 'lovely water'.

**Talitha**
Aramaic, meaning 'young girl'.

**Tallulah**
*(alt. Taliyah)*
Native American, meaning 'leaping water'.

**Tamara**
*(alt. Tamera)*
Hebrew, meaning 'palm tree'.

T

## Tamatha
*(alt. Tametha)*
American, meaning 'dear Tammy'.

## Tamika
*(alt. Tameka)*
American, meaning 'people'.

## Tammy
*(alt. Tami, Tammie)*
Shortened form of Tamsin, meaning 'twin'.

## Tamsin
Hebrew, meaning 'twin'.

## Tanis
Spanish, meaning 'to make famous'.

## Tanya
*(alt. Tania, Tanya, Tonya)*
Shortened form of Tatiana, meaning 'from the Tatius clan'.

## Tara
*(alt. Tarah, Tera)*
Irish Gaelic, meaning 'rocky hill'.

## Tasha
*(alt. Taisha, Tarsha)*
Shortened form of Natasha, meaning 'Christmas'.

## Tatiana
*(alt. Tayana)*
Russian, meaning 'from the Tatius clan'.

## Tatum
English, meaning 'light-hearted'.

## Tawny
*(alt. Tawanaa, Tawnee, Tawnya)*
English, meaning 'golden brown'.

## Taya
Greek, meaning 'poor one'.

## Taylor
*(alt. Tayler)*
English, meaning 'tailor'.

## Tea
Greek, meaning 'goddess'.

**T**

## Teagan
(alt. *Teague, Tegan*)
Irish Gaelic, meaning 'poet'.

## Teal
English, from the bird of the same name.

## Tecla
Greek, meaning 'fame of God'.

## Temperance
English, meaning 'virtue'.

## Tempest
French, meaning 'storm'.

## Teresa
(alt. *Terese, Theresa, Therese*)
Greek, meaning 'harvest'.

## Terry
(alt. *Teri, Terrie*)
Shortened form of Teresa, meaning 'harvest'.

## Tessa
(alt. *Tess, Tessie*)
Shortened form of Teresa, meaning 'harvest'.

## Thais
Greek, from the mythological heroine of the same name.

## Thalia
Greek, meaning 'blooming'.

## Thandi
(alt. *Thana*)
Arabic, meaning 'thanksgiving'.

## Thea
Greek, meaning 'goddess'.

## Theda
German, meaning 'people'.

## Thelma
Greek, meaning 'will'.

## Theodora
Greek, meaning 'gift of God'.

## Theodosia
Greek, meaning 'gift of God'.

## Thisbe
Greek, from the mythological heroine of the same name.

T

## Thomasina
(alt. Thomasin, Thomasine, Thomasyn)
Greek, meaning 'twin'.

## Thora
Scandinavian, meaning 'Thor's struggle'.

## Tia
(alt. Tiana)
Spanish, meaning 'aunt'.

## Tiara
Latin, meaning 'jewelled headband'.

## Tierney
Irish Gaelic, meaning 'Lord'.

## Tierra
(alt. Tiera)
Spanish, meaning 'land'.

## Tiffany
(alt. Tiffani, Tiffanie)
Greek, meaning 'God's appearance'.

## Tiggy
Shortened form of Tigris, meaning 'tiger'.

## Tigris
Irish Gaelic, meaning 'tiger'.

## Tilda
Shortened form of Matilda, meaning 'battle-mighty'.

## Tillie
(alt. Tilly)
Shortened form of Matilda, meaning 'battle-mighty'.

## Timothea
Greek, meaning 'honoring God'.

## Tina
(alt. Teena, Tena)
Shortened form of Christina, meaning 'anointed Christian'.

## Tirion
Welsh, meaning 'kind and gentle'.

## Tirzah
Hebrew, meaning 'pleasantness'.

## Titania
Greek, meaning 'giant'.

T

## Toby
*(alt. Tobi)*

Hebrew, meaning 'God is good'.

## Toni
*(alt. Tony)*

Latin, meaning 'invaluable'.

## Tonia
*(alt. Tonja, Tonya)*

Russian, meaning 'praiseworthy'.

## Topaz

Latin, meaning 'golden gemstone'.

## Tori
*(alt. Tora)*

Shortened form of Victoria, meaning 'victory'.

## Autumn names

Autumn
Demetria
September
Theresa
Tracey

## Tova
*(alt. Tovah, Tove)*

Hebrew, meaning 'good'.

## Tracy
*(alt. Tracey, Tracie)*

Greek, meaning 'harvest'.

## Treva

Welsh, meaning 'homestead'.

## Tricia

Shortened form of Patricia, meaning 'aristocratic'.

## Trilby

English, meaning 'vocal trills'.

## Trina
*(alt. Trena)*

Greek, meaning 'pure'.

## Trinity

Latin, meaning 'triad'.

## Trisha

Shortened form of Patricia, meaning 'noble'.

## Trista

Latin, meaning 'sad'.

**T**

### Trixie

Shortened form of Beatrix, meaning 'bringer of gladness'.

### Trudy

*(alt. Tru, Trudie)*

Shortened form of Gertrude, meaning 'strength of a spear'.

### Tullia

Spanish, meaning 'bound for glory'.

### Twyla

*(alt. Twila)*

American, meaning 'star'.

### Tyler

English, meaning 'tiler'.

### Tyra

Scandinavian, meaning 'Thor's struggle'.

### Tzipporah

Hebrew, meaning 'bird'.

## Popular Spanish names for boys and girls

Carmen
Catalina
Diego
Esmeralda
Jesus
José
Juanita
Miguel
Ramona
Santiago

**T**

# U Girls' names

### Ula
*(alt. Ulla)*
Celtic, meaning 'gem of the sea'.

### Ulrika
*(alt. Urica)*
German, meaning 'power of the wolf'.

### Uma
Sanskrit, meaning 'flax'.

### Una
Latin, meaning 'one'.

### Undine
Latin, meaning 'little wave'.

## Winter names

January
Neva
Neve
Perdita
Rainer
Tahoma

### Unice
Greek, meaning 'victorious'.

### Unique
Latin, meaning 'only one'.

### Unity
English, meaning 'oneness'.

## Uriela

Hebrew, meaning 'God's light'.

## Ursula

Latin, meaning 'little female bear'.

## Uta

German, meaning 'prospers in battle'.

# V

# Girls' names

## Vada

German, meaning 'famous ruler'.

## Vale

Shortened form of Valencia, meaning 'strong and healthy'.

## Valencia

*(alt. Valancy, Valarece)*

Latin, meaning 'strong and healthy'.

## Valentina

Latin, meaning 'strong and healthy'.

## Valentine

Latin, from the saint of the same name.

## Valeria

Latin, meaning 'to be healthy and strong'.

## Valerie

*(alt. Valarie, Valery, Valorie)*

Latin, meaning 'to be healthy and strong'.

## Valia

*(alt. Vallie)*

Shortened form of Valerie, meaning 'to be healthy and strong'.

## Vandana

Sanskrit, meaning 'worship'.

## Vanessa

*(alt. Vanesa)*

English, from the *Gulliver's Travels* character of the same name.

## Vanity

Latin, meaning 'self-obsessed'.

## Vashti

Persian, meaning 'beauty'.

## Veda

Sanskrit, meaning 'knowledge and wisdom'.

## Vega

Arabic, meaning 'falling vulture'.

## Velda

German, meaning 'ruler'.

## Vella

American, meaning 'beautiful'.

## Velma

English, meaning 'determined protector'.

## Venice

*(alt. Venetia, Venita)*

Latin, meaning 'city of canals'. From the city of the same name.

## Venus

Latin, from the Roman goddess of the same name.

## Vera

*(alt. Verla, Verlie)*

Slavic, meaning 'faith'.

## Verda

*(alt. Verdie)*

Latin, meaning 'spring-like'.

## Verena

Latin, meaning 'true'.

## Verity

Latin, meaning 'truth'.

## Verna

*(alt. Vernie)*

Latin, meaning 'spring green'.

## Verona

Latin, shortened form of Veronica. From the city of the same name.

## Christmas names

Carol
Eve
Gloria
Holly
Ivy
Mary
Natasha
Noël
Robin

**Veronica**

*(alt. Verica, Veronique)*

Latin, meaning 'true image'.

**Veruca**

Latin, meaning 'wart'.

**Vesta**

Latin, from the Roman goddess of the same name.

**Vicenta**

Latin, meaning 'prevailing'.

**Vicky**

*(alt. Vicki, Vikki, Vix)*

Shortened form of Victoria, meaning 'victory'.

**Victoria**

Latin, meaning 'victory'.

**Vida**

Spanish, meaning 'life'.

**Vidya**

Sanskrit, meaning 'knowledge'.

**Vienna**

Latin, from the city of the same name.

**Vigdis**

Scandinavian, meaning 'war goddess'.

**Vina**

*(alt. Vena)*

Spanish, meaning 'vineyard'.

**Viola**

Latin, meaning 'violet'.

**Violet**

*(alt. Violetta)*

Latin, meaning 'purple'.

**Virgie**

Shortened form of Virginia, meaning 'maiden'.

## Virginia
*(alt. Virginie)*
Latin, meaning 'maiden'.

## Vita
Latin, meaning 'life'.

## Vittoria
Variation of Victoria, meaning 'victory'.

## Viva
Latin, meaning 'alive'.

## Viveca
Scandinavian, meaning 'war fortress'.

## Vivian
*(alt. Vivien, Vivienne)*
Latin, meaning 'lively'.

## Vonda
Czech, meaning 'from the tribe of Vandals'.

## Food-inspired names

Anise
Candy
Cherry
Coco
Ginger
Honey
Meena
Olive
Saffron

# Girls' names

## Waleska
Polish, meaning 'beautiful'.

## Wallis
English, meaning 'from Wales'.

## Wanda
*(alt. Waneta, Wanita)*
Slavic, meaning 'tribe of the vandals'.

## Waneta
Variation of Wanda meaning 'tribe of the vandals'.

## Wanita
Variation of Wanda meaning 'tribe of the vandals'.

## Wava
English, meaning 'way'.

## Waverly
*(alt. Waverley)*
Old English, meaning 'meadow of aspens'.

## Wendy
English, meaning 'friend'.

## Whisper
English, meaning 'whisper'.

## Whitley
Old English, meaning 'white meadow'.

## Whitney
Old English, meaning 'white island'.

## Wilda
German, meaning 'willow tree'.

## Wilhelmina
German, meaning 'determined'.

## Willene
*(alt. Willa, Willia)*
German, meaning 'helmet'.

## Willow
English, from the tree of the same name.

## Wilma
German, meaning 'protection'.

## Winifred
Old English, meaning 'holy and blessed'.

## Winnie
Shortened form of Winifred, meaning 'holy and blessed'.

## Winona
*(alt. Wynona)*
Indian, meaning 'first-born daughter'.

## Winslow
English, meaning 'friend's hill'.

## Winter
English, meaning 'winter'.

## Wisteria
English, meaning 'flower'.

## Wren
English, meaning 'wren'.

## Wynne
Welsh, meaning 'white'.

### Bird names
Ava
Oriole
Raven
Teal
Wren

# X Girls' names

**Xanthe**
Greek, meaning 'blonde'.

**Xanthippe**
Greek, meaning 'nagging'.

**Xaverie**
Greek, meaning 'bright'.

**Xaviera**
Arabic, meaning 'bright'.

**Xena**
Greek, meaning 'foreigner'.

**Xenia**
Greek, meaning 'foreigner'.

**Ximena**
Greek, meaning 'listening'.

**Xiomara**
Spanish, meaning 'battle-ready'.

**Xochitl**
Spanish, meaning 'flower'.

**Xoey**
Variation of Zoe, meaning 'life'.

**Xristina**
Variation of Christina, meaning 'follower of Christ'.

**Xylia**
(alt. Xylina, Xyloma)
Greek, meaning 'from the woods'.

## Popular Welsh names for boys and girls

| | |
|---|---|
| Bronwen | Ioan |
| Cerys | Myfanwy |
| Dafydd | Owain |
| Dylan | Rhys |
| Gwynn | Siân |

# Y Girls' names

### Yadira
Arabic, meaning 'worthy'.

### Yael
Hebrew, meaning 'mountain goat'.

### Yaffa
*(alt. Yahaira, Yajaira)*
Hebrew, meaning lovely.

### Yamilet
Arabic, meaning 'beautiful'.

### Yana
Hebrew, meaning 'the Lord is gracious'.

### Yanira
Hawaiian, meaning 'pretty'.

### Yareli
Latin, meaning 'golden'.

### Yaretzi
*(alt. Yaritza)*
Hawaiian, meaning 'forever beloved'.

### Yasmin
*(alt. Yasmeen, Yasmina)*
Persian, meaning 'jasmine flower'.

### Yelena
Greek, meaning 'bright and chosen'.

### Yesenia
Arabic, meaning 'flower'.

## Yetta

English, from Henrietta, meaning 'ruler of the house'.

## Yeva

Hebrew variant of Eve, meaning 'life'.

## Ylva

Old Norse, meaning 'sea wolf'.

## Yoki

(alt. Yoko)

Native American, meaning 'rain'.

## Yolanda

(alt. Yolonda)

Spanish, meaning 'violet flower'.

## Yoselin

English, meaning 'lovely'.

## Yoshiko

Japanese, meaning 'good child'.

## Ysabel

English, meaning 'God's promise'.

---

## Names from nature

Acacia
Amaryllis
Dahlia
Juniper
Primrose

---

## Ysanne

Contraction of Isabel and Anne, meaning 'pledged to God' and 'grace'.

## Yuki

Japanese, meaning 'lucky'.

## Yuliana

Latin, meaning 'youthful'.

## Yuridia

Russian, meaning 'farmer'.

## Yvette

(alt. Yvonne)

French, meaning 'yew'.

**Y**

# Z Girls' names

**Zafira**

Arabic, meaning 'successful'.

**Zahara**

*(alt. Zahava, Zahra)*

Arabic, meaning 'flowering and shining'.

**Zaida**

*(alt. Zaide)*

Arabic, meaning 'prosperous'.

**Zalika**

Swahili, meaning 'well born'.

**Zaltana**

Arabic, meaning 'high mountain'.

**Zamia**

Greek, meaning 'pine cone'.

**Zaniyah**

Arabic, meaning 'lily'.

**Zara**

*(alt. Zaria, Zariah, Zora)*

Arabic, meaning 'radiance'.

**Zelda**

German, meaning 'dark battle'.

**Zelia**

*(alt. Zella)*

Scandinavian, meaning 'sunshine'.

**Zelma**

German, meaning 'helmet'.

**Zemirah**

Hebrew, meaning 'joyous melody'.

**Zena**
(alt. Zenia, Zina)
Greek, meaning 'hospitable'.

**Zenaida**
Greek, meaning 'the life of Zeus'.

**Zenobia**
Latin, meaning 'the life of Zeus'.

**Zetta**
Italian, meaning 'Z'.

**Zia**
Arabic, meaning 'light and splendor'.

**Zinaida**
Greek, meaning 'belonging to Zeus'.

**Zinnia**
Latin, meaning 'flower'.

**Zipporah**
Hebrew, meaning 'bird'.

**Zita**
(alt. Ziva)
Spanish, meaning 'little girl'.

**Zoe**
Greek, meaning 'life'.

**Zoila**
Greek, meaning 'life'.

**Zoraida**
Spanish, meaning 'captivating woman'.

**Zosia**
(alt. Zosima)
Greek, meaning 'wisdom'.

**Zoya**
Greek, meaning 'life'.

**Zula**
African, meaning 'brilliant'.

**Zuleika**
Arabic, meaning 'fair and intelligent'.

**Zulma**
Arabic, meaning 'peace'.

**Zuzana**
Hebrew, meaning 'lily'.

**Zuzu**
Czech, meaning 'flower'.

**Z**